SPIRIT - FILLED

SERMON OUTLINES

From A to Z

VOLUME ONE

Dr Michael h Yeager

 All Scripture quotations, unless otherwise indicated, are taken from the King James Authorized Version of the Bible.

(Some of the teaching in this book is partly taken from the Adam Clarke Commentary, and other non-copy right or copy right acknowledged material found on the internet)

ISBN: 9781075415654
Imprint: Independently published

DEDICATION

All of the Scriptures used in this meditation book is from the original 1611 version of the King James Bible. I give thanks to God the Father , Jesus Christ and the Holy Ghost for the powerful impact the word has had upon my life. Without the word Quicken in my heart by the Holy Ghost I would've been lost and I'm done. To the Lord of Heaven and Earth I am eternally indebted for his great love and his mercy, his protections and his provisions, his divine guidance and overwhelming goodness. To him be glory and praise for ever and ever: Amen .

***Notice: There will be some repetition in this book. Please do not be offended by this fact.**

CONTENTS

ACKNOWLEDGMENTS

*To our heavenly Father and His wonderful love.

*To our Lord, Savior and Master —Jesus Christ, Who saved us and set us free because of His great love for us.

*To the Holy Spirit, Who leads and guides us into the realm of miraculous living every day.

*To all of those who had a part in helping us get this book ready for the publishers.

*To our precious children, Michael, Daniel, Steven, Stephanie, Catherine Yu, who is our precious daughter-in-law, and Naomi, who is now with the Lord.

CHAPTER ONE

Importance of This Book

This book is written to equip you to do battle. Every **SERMON OUTLINE** and Scripture I share in this book is with the intent of being **STUDIED** and **Meditated** upon and to **Minister** to **Others**. In order for you to enjoy the victory that **Christ Jesus** has already obtained for you, it is necessary for you to hide the **TRUTH** in your **heart**. These truths, these realities are an accumulation of over 40 years of Study within **God's WORD** and inspirations of the **Holy Ghost**!

There are over **7000 promises** alone given to the believer in the word of God. The Sermon Outlines I share in this book are a very small portion of some of those wonderful, exceedingly great, and precious truths. I cannot cover in this one book well over **5000 Sermon Out Lines** I have written over the years.

***Please take these Sermons & Scriptures seriously!**

ABILITY - OUT LINES

ABILITY: GOD GIVETH -- NUMBER 1

I PETER 4:10-11

ABILITY To exercise force, to have power!

GRACE God's unmerited ability. Imagine the infinite power of God, with that awesome power the planners and stars were created. The earth was formed and man was brought forth upon it!

Same limitless power is locked up in your inner man, waiting to be released! You have God's ability in you just waiting for it to manifest.

Our worst enemy is our self. We limit God, or allow Him to be limitless in us!

ZEC 4:6 **Not by might, nor by power, but by my Spirit, saith the Lord!** If you choose to face life by yourself, God will let you go it above. He respects your freedom to decide your own spiritual destiny. (Flesh won't do the job)

CHRISTIANITY Supernatural walk, supernatural way of life.

I COR 2:1-5 **(:4 :5)** Depended on God, Period! Paul: no confidence in flesh!

"Had education university of Tarsus." *Workers.

2 COR 6:1 **Vain**. The presence of God's awesome power does you little good if you do not allow that power to work in and through you. A lot never release God's ability? Are you too lazy to seek God?

ONE DAY AT A TIME

THE GOD GIVEN ABILITY -- NUMBER 2

I PETER 4:10-11, 2 PETER 1:2-3, EPHESIANS 6:10
I CORINTHIANS 15:10 2 PETER 3:18

I PET 4:10-11 Minister. Serve, wait upon. Ability. Have or exercise force. Not our ability. Respond to His ability. "Let Him do it through you" (God created, indwelt, empowered, led) Same miracle working power manifested in Jesus imparted in us. "Not by power nor might but by my Spirit, God".

II PET 1:2-3 Grace is unmerited ability. God abounding. Knowledge not information (spare tire) I **AM, I HAVE, I CAN.**

EPH 6:10 In Lord, "Won't get ahead leaving GOD behind." You only conquer life to the extent that you contact God (See self as God sees)

Psychological barriers. Example: Elephant. God wants us to soar like eagles, but many Christians are content to scratch like chickens. Devil knows you can, so says He you cannot.

I COR 15:10 Yet not I. Die to Self like, esteem, confidence, for Jesus to increase. Kingdom not built on leftovers. Consuming fire, clothed in power. Only flow to extent of Word in Life.

2 PET 3:18 Grow. Enlarge, increase amplify.

Stop wrestling with the Word of God and start resting. Ever going to accomplish anything. Have to be in God's ability.

1 Peter 4:10-11

:10 "Every man". Minister: Serve, wait upon! One to another. World put's itself first. We put God first and ourselves last.

:11 In God's ability, to have or exercise force! Not your ability, why so many never do anything. Realize already have God's ability and that you do not have to be a big shot to set free. Why? Found out step out in faith. Example: Peter on water. "God's ability" People struggle.

2 Peter 1:2-3 Grace: Gods unmerited ability. His-has (ability) all things (repeat) doesn't want us to know. Do not pray something you have! Admit: I have what the Bible says I have and I am etc. "All Jesus is and did is ours."

Eph 6:10 In the Lord, not self. You decide. You can "devil" knows you can so he says you can't. See yourself as God see you! Refuse to see anything else.

Luke 9:61&62 Looking back. Past life, faults, inabilities, weaknesses. Old man gone. New creation! New species of man. For your information: effective. World: Be reasonable and sensible. No lets be Bible. We are God created, God indwelt, God empowered, and God led.

ONE WAY, ONE JOB; JESUS AND SOUL WINNING!

I Peter 4:10-11

I Peter 4:10-11 **Ability**. To have or exercise force. Grace: God's unmerited favor and ability. "I am what God's word says I am" God created, indwelt, empowered, led. See yourself as God sees you.

Gift. Special spiritual enablement's! God given abilities. It is God who is at work in you. The devil knows you can, so he says you cannot.

I Cor 15:9-10 I AM what I AM "Moses, Joshua, David, Jonathan, Samson, Elijah, etc. The miracle working power that was manifested in Jesus, is now imparted in us. Not in vain and not useless. I cannot do anything. But I know someone who can through me.

Eph 3: 7-8 Paul ministered in God's ability!

I Peter 5:5-7 Proud. God gives grace to the humble. Thinks or tries to do it in himself! Humble: "Esteeming yourself small in as much as we are so, and therefore being completely dependent on God and receiving all we need from HIM."

Christian suffer today because they try to do it on their own.

2 Peter 3:10 **Grow**. Enlarge, increase, and amplify. Grace and knowledge is God. It flows from God through us.

THE GOD GIVEN ABILITY -- NUMBER 3

I PETER 4:10-11 ZEC 4:6

Realize God is not asking you to do His works but let Him do them through you.

See only what He says -- will put you over every time! "Renewing mind" Example: Psychological barriers: Elephants, pest, (new way of life) natural man cannot. (Mind of devil) You can through Jesus!

JHN 1:14-17 Jesus is full of grace and truth. Word and God's ability. You conquer life to the extent that you have contact with God.

:16 Fullness we received! (Yours, use it) Example: Brains, use them. "Grace for Grace"

:17 By Jesus Christ and Him crucified! "To fulfill Law" People give up to easily and become lazy. Learning to lean.

ACT 4:33 Great grace? Only manifested when act on God's Word in faith. Do not settle for less. I do not want to just possess faith. Faith possesses me. Jesus = Jesus.

I TIM 1:12 Faithful to use God's ability. No one is predestined for defeat or failure. Place your life in to the hands of God. Do not have faith in yourself or man but in God.

DAN 11:32 Shall be strong and do exploits.

THE GOD GIVEN ABILITY -- NUMBER 4

I PETER 4:10-11

When we stop, Jesus will start!

God's given us His ability. (God created indwelt, empowered, and led) Glorified. Only God! No way can brag.

2 COR 3:5,6 Think anything of selves! You're not sufficient. Our sufficiency is God! Period. What we are and have is in Christ. Spirit giveth life. Not by might nor by power, but by my Spirit says Lord of Host. Flesh profits nothing.

GAL 3:1-5 Made perfect by flesh? No! Ability flows by faith.

I COR 4,7 We must decrease in self-like, self-esteem, self-confidence, for Jesus to increase! God only promotes people He can trust.

I COR 15:10 By the grace of God I AM what I AM.

ALL THE GLORY GOES TO GOD.

Ever going to accomplish anything it is going to have to be in God's ability.

THE GOD GIVEN ABILITY NUMBER 5

I PET 4:10-11 Flows from God through us to mankind. Ability: To have or exercise force. Grace is God's unmerited ability.

:10 Every move. Get eyes off of self. Trust in Lord.

I'll speak; major key releasing God's ability. Must hear to manifest. Words of mouth -- fruits of thoughts.

Let God created indwelt, empowered, and led. Limitless, locked up inside. Devil knows we can so he says you cannot. I AM because God is (see yourself as God sees) Limit God or Be limitless?

II TIM 2:20-21 **Vessel**: Instrument, tool, and equipment. Certain job.

PURGE Clears, purify, remove impurities or contamination. Mind number 1 area Christians defeated in.

THINGS Iniquity. Anything that is not of faith!

HIMSELF God will not purge you, He will help you. Your decision.

SANCTIFY Set apart, yielded to God for purpose of fulfilling His will on face of earth.

MEET Appropriate, suitable

PREPARED Ready, available

II TIM 3:16&17 The ability of God can only flow in my life to the extent that you allow God's word to control your life. Example: Kite with wind

BROKEN HUMANITY

DOES GOD CARE?

MR 4:35 - LU 2:1-7

MR 4:35-38 Picture yourself in their place! * In the will of God? Yes, others also!
:37 Greater violent storm, Why? **JOB 5:6,7** -Although affliction cometh not forth of the dust, neither doth -trouble spring out of the ground; yet man is born

unto trouble, as -the sparks fly upward.

SINKING, SWAMPED, (Where is Jesus? A sleep) Looks like will drown, perish, die. {Awoke him with these words} ** **CAREST NOT** = Indifferent, unconcerned, gives a rip. No skin off my nose! Example Humanity=drowning, hurting, bleeding, wounded, sick, tormented, famines, earthquakes, pestilence, floods, mudslides, volcanic eruptions, murders, rapes, divorce, plagues, cancer, aids (steeped to lips in misery) **"WHERE IS GOD" {IN SAME BOAT}** *God does care -- doesn't respond same way **:39**

I **JOB 30:25** did not I weep for him that was in trouble? Was not my soul grieved for the poor? **LU 13:34** How often I would have gathered thy children together as a hen doeth gather her brood under her wings and ye would not. Same boat! **ISA 63:9** in all their affliction. He was afflicted.

LUKE 2:1-7

:40 Why are you such cowards? No faith = have not yet. **:41** were awestruck weather days, but men won't. **LU 2:1-5** Taxed (greed) oppression of innocent! Great with child! Discomfort, rough, possible miscarriage. -- Lost of Life, **:7** No room, = no room, = not hot water, or bed or warmeth, wrapped in rags, trough for crib. Did God care? Where is he? Couldn't provide better? *Walking in our shoes! **JER 10:19** Woe is me for my hurt! My wound is grievous. --But I said truly this a grief and must bear it.

***Birth of Christ is God's declaration, I care, your special to me valuable precious.**

HEB 4:14-16

HEB 4:14-16, He's not unable, not incapable to sympathize with our infirmities, hurts, wounds. In every way tempted and tried, but yet without SIN! **PS 40:17** But I am poor and needy. Yet the Lord thinketh upon me, thou are my help and my deliver. Make no tarrying my God.

HELPING THE HURTING -- NUMBER 2

More hurting today like never before! Jeremiah sent to help, restore, heal, deliver Israel = sick, wounded, suffering, tormented nation. **Like America!

I **JER 14:17-19**. Notice their condition! **JER 30:12** For thus saith the Lord, thy bruise is incurable and they wound is grievous. (52 chapters)

II Process -- pathway -- line of action! Jeremiah outlines it!

III Admit hurting (like adultery) don't deny. **REV 3:17** Wretched, miserable, poor, blind, naked. Listen to songs, out of mouth, Look!!! Fruit you will eat. **JER 2:13** Cisterns, broken cisterns, which cannot hold water. Gone after emptiness, fantasies, falsehoods, futility! {Sounds like USA}

IV Why hurting? **JER 5:1** Sin **ISA 1:5** Why should you be stricken anymore? Yes, will revolt more and more! The whole head is sick and the whole heart faint. **PS 107:17** Fools because of their transgressions and because of their iniquities are afflicted. National SIN = wicked, forsaken God, indifferent to God no fear of judgment, unfaithful, disobedient. {Kept declaring innocent} "through whole book".

JER 6:14

V **JER 6:14** Slightly = insignificantly, over so little, make shift provision, quick fix, bubble gum and bailing wire, (bandaid on broken arm, aspirin for cut throat)
* The world declares it has the answers! Deceived!

JER 13:17

VI **JER 13:17** Weeping prophet, (Lamentations) grieve, sorrow, cry out! **JHN 11:35** Jesus wept. **ISA 63:9** In all their afflictions, he was afflicted.

JER14:20-22

VII **JERE 14:20-22**. Acknowledge SIN! **JAMES 4:8-10**.

JAMES 4:8-10

VIII **JAMES 4:8-10**. He will make your lives significant. **PS 41:4** ***I said Lord, be merciful unto me! Heal my soul: for I have sinned against thee.*** **JER 3:13**

Only know, understand, acknowledge, your iniquities, rebellion, transgression and guilt against God.

JER 30:17 I WILL HEAL!

ALL THINGS POSSIBLE

GAL 3:5, I JHN 5: 13, 14 & 15, I JHN 3:22, MR 9:17-27, MR 11:22, 14

GAL 3:5 Miracles an event, action that apparently contradicts known scientific Laws, extraordinary, supernatural in origin and character. *{Something you need to happen that is beyond you present ability or resources} I need some miracles. **ACTS 6:6-8** **GAL 3:5** He -- whosoever, miracles by faith. **ACTS 6:8** Steven, full of faith and power, did great wonders and miracles among the people. Greatest demand. 5 absolutes. [1] Must know the will of God.

1 JHN 5:14&15

[II] **1 JOHN 5:14 & 15**. Confidence, anything, His will. [2] Plug into God **JHN 15:7**, if ye abide in me, and my Word in You. [3] **WORD.** **ROM 10:17**, Faith cometh by hearing etc.

[III] **I JHN 5:13** Written that you may believe.

[IV] [4] Praying in Spirit -- **JUDE 20** [5] Do, obey, put to practice, **JAM 1:22.** *Use shield of faith against temptations!

1 JHN 3:22

[V] **I JHN 3:22** Because, keep *Christianity is demonstration of the righteousness of God. {Takes faith to not Sin} **2 COR 10:4&5** ***Weapons of our warfare...*** **EPH 6:16** ***Above all, taking shield of faith, where with ye...*** *Faith is a major protection against devil, sickness etc. Satan wants to rob our faith (confidence, trust, hope, commitment) by --- worldly, devilish, earthly things. Ex: **HEB 11** Woe to the devil if we ever get serious with God. Satan wants to fill our minds with doubt, to steal our precious faith.

I PET 1:7 ***That the trial of your faith being much more precious than of gold, that perisheth, though it be tried with fire, might be found unto praise and honor and glory at the appearing of Jesus Christ.*** **HEB 12:2** ***Looking unto Jesus the author and finisher of faith.***

MRK 11:22

[VI] **MR 9:17-27.** **:18** Brags and boast **:21** How long? **:22** Boast **:19** Faithless generation (We limit Holy One of Israel) **:23** Art able, whatsoever things, (We limit God) Everything is possible for the one who has faith "in Jesus" **:25** Rebuked by saying = Rebuke and will lose you. Charge = command

MR 11:22

VII **MRK 11:22 [:14]** Faith of God {confidence} **:23** As many as -- say, move it, = calls by name. And does not waver, no inward doubts, hesitate. Believe -- persuaded, confident. **:24** Come to be, fulfilled.

YOUR CONFESSION IS THE EXPRESSION OF WHAT YOU BELIEVE. GOD HAS NEVER DONE ANYTHING WITHOUT SAYING IT FIRST.

ANOINTED VESSELS

ISA 64:8, JER 18:2-6, 2 KINGS 2:18-15

Our divine purpose, objective, Master's plan. A deep mysterious plan. ***I COR 2:9 eyes have not seen***. **Once we get a glimpse -- will motivate, compel, drive us on, energize us.

ISA 64:8 Clay - reddish mud, slime, mire. ***JAMES 4:7 Submit yourself***. **GEN 2:7** We are the dust of the earth. Without the potter's touch, that's all you will ever be compared to what you could be. **Potter** - He forms, fashions, shapes, molds, according to the purpose He has in mind for you.

** God is totally committed to the success of His product. Work - Hand - What God has called you to be cannot be done without His hands. **PHIL 1:6** ***Being confident of this...*** **JER 18:1-6** **:3.** Wrought a work. We are on the wheel. **Marred** = **:4** to stiff, dry, a stone. What the potter can do with you is determined by what you are made out of. **2 TIM 2:20,21** But in a great way, God wants us to soar like eagles, but many Christians are content to scratch like chickens. **Rework** = Add water (spirit)! Does what He can! **2 KINGS 2:8** Elijah - 1) Mighty 2) Jehovah **Mantle** = Anointing. **ACTS 10:38** You know of Jesus. **I JHN 3:8** **LU 4:18** {always used supernatural to shape people}

:9 Ask - **First** a) heard the call, b) forsook, c) followed, d) served, e) refused to turn back. **Saw** = **:10-12** Had a revelation of God, His man and His plan. **ACTS 7:55**. Stephen saw glory of God, and Jesus on right side. **Rent clothes:** His old life, ideas, plans, entered a new realm, up to this moment a spectator! **A man at his best, apart from God, is but a weakling.

:13 Mantle = you will take a hold of the anointing. Step into the cloak of the anointing. **:9** double. **JHN 14:12** The works that I do before this a normal man. **2 COR 4:7** ***But we have this treasure in earthen vessels, that the excellency of the power may be of God and not of us.*** The anointing that flowing through Jesus now flow through us. It is the source, origin, essence of our success in fulfilling our purpose. **HEB 11:34,35** ***Who subdued kingdoms***....

BLOOD, FIRE, AND VAPOR THE MIGHTY HAND OF GOD

ACTS 2:14-21 :16

ACTS 2:14-21 That which = NOW, this moment, until return of Christ to earth. [1] **Filled with Spirit** = controlled, moved, overflowing, set a flame, {Something happens when Spirit and filled} **:15** Not drunken -- Looked drunk, intoxicated.

[2] **Supernatural abilities** = gifts of Holy Ghost, unctions. [3] **Visions**. Dreams, divine insight Peter, Paul, John. [4] Signs **:19, 20** [5] Salvation. *Last day's, not only, technology break through, natural advances. But supernatural. ***ISA 40:5 & the glory of the Lord shall be revealed and all flesh shall see it together for the mouth of the Lord hath spoken it.*** [Much of it God -- some of it devil] **Must** = Not be paranoid. Ex: = Tongues of devil. ***2 TIM 1:7 God has not given a spirit of fear but of a sound mind***. *3 major points

[I] **I JHN 4:1** ***Beloved believer not every spirit, but try out...*** **:2** Jesus came in flesh "should have inner witness, not our heads" Carnal mind cannot understand! Not contradict, word, or nature! {Earthly ministry -- Pharisees, Sadducees, adamant man of Word! They declared Jesus, was of devil! Not lined up with their interpretation scriptures. [Contradicted laws of Leviticus, picked food, and healed and had people work on Sabbath day--Trinity]. *Absolute, outright, arbitrary disobedience -- in their understanding.* (He was wrong or they were) Ex: Same today. Seduction of Christianity! Wrong spirit. Wanted to kill Jesus, disciples -- no love, burn at stake.

2 TIM 3:1 Perilous days. **:5** Form of Godliness, denying = strangers to God's power. **I THES 5:19** **Quench not the Spirit** = Do not stifle what God is doing. **:20** Prophesying **:21** Prove all things = test, hold fast = retain only what is good. *[Don't make a big deal].

[III] **Bottom line** = Changed lives, fruit of the spirit and people being saved.

ACTS 4:29

ACTS 4:29:30 Thine hand = signs, wonders, miracles. [They asked - we asked] Why? Multitudes got saved. **:31** Shaken = moved violently, rocked to and fro **:33** Got power **5:12** By the hands = signs, wonders.

LUKE 4:18 Anointed = divine impartation by the laying on of hands. **I TIM 4:14** ***Neglect not the gift that is in thee . . . 2 TIM 1:6 Wherefore I put thee etc.*** The same miracle working power that was in Jesus and his hands is in us!

LUK 10:19 ***Behold I give unto you power .... ACTS 11:21 The hand of the Lord was with them; a great number believed and turned unto the Lord.***

2DEUT 26:7

DEUT 26:7,8,9. ***I PET 5:6 Humble yourselves therefore under the mighty hand of God; that he may exalt you in due time!***

EXO 8:5

EXO 8:5 Your hand. **9:22** Your hand = creative ability, skill, talent, craftsmanship.
:33 Got power **5:12** By the hands = signs, wonders. ***2 SAM 22:35 He teacheth my hands to war so that a bow of steel is broken by mine arms.***

BLOOD, FIRE, AND VAPOR #2
THE MIGHTY HAND OF GOD

ACTS 2:14-21 :16 That which = NOW, this moment, until return of Christ to earth.
1. Filled with Spirit=controlled, moved, flame, {Something happens when Spirit and filled}

:15 drunken -- Looked drunk, intoxicated.

2. Supernatural abilities = Gifts of Holy Ghost, unctions.

3. Visions, dreams, divine insight Peter, Paul, John.

4. Signs = :19, 20

5. Salvation

Last day's, not only, technology break through, natural advances. But supernatural Isa 40:5 & the glory of the Lord shall be revealed and all flesh shall see it together for the mouth of the Lord hath spoken it. [Much of it God -- Some of it Devil]
MUST Not be paranoid. Examples = Tongues of devil.

2 Tim 1:7 God has not given a spirit of fear but of a sound mind.

3Major Points

A.I Jhn 4:1 Beloved believer not every spirit, but try out... :2Jesus came in flesh "should have inner witness, not our heads" Carnal, mind cannot understand!

B. Not contradict, word, or nature! {Earthly ministry -- pharisees, sadducees, adamant man of Word! They declared Jesus, was of devil! Not lined up with their interpretation scriptures.

[Contradict laws of Leviticus, picked food, and healed and had people work on Sabbath day--Trinity. *Absolute, outright, arbitrary disobedience -- in their understanding. He was wrong or they were) Example: Same today =Seduction of Christianity! Wrong Spirit. Wanted to kill Jesus, disciples -- no Love, burn at stake., 2 Tim 3:1 perilous days.

:5Form of Godliness, denying = strangers to God's power.

I Thes 5:19 Quench not the Spirit = Do not stifle what God is doing.

:20 Prophesying

:21 Prove all things = test, hold fast = retain only what is good. Do not make a big deal.

Acts 4:29 Bottom line = Changed lives, fruit of the spirit and people being saved.

Acts 4:29:30 Thine hand = signs, wonders, miracles. [They asked - we asked] Why? Multitudes got saved.

: 31Shaken = moved violently, rocked to and fro

: 33Got power

5:12 By the hands = signs, wonders.

Lu 4:18 Anointed = divine impartation by the laying on of hands.

I Tim 4:14 Neglect not the gift that is in thee

2 Tim 1:6 Wherefore I put thee etc.
The same miracle working power that was in Jesus and his hands is in us!
Lu 10:19 Behold I give unto you power **Acts 11:21**

Deut 26:7. The hand of the Lord was with them; a great number believed and turned unto the Lord.

Deut 26:7,8,9

I Peter 5:6 Humble yourselves therefore under the mighty hand of God; that he may exalt you in due time!

Exodus 8:5Your hand. 9:22 Your hand = creative ability, skill, talent, craftsmanship.

2 Sam 22:35He teacheth my hands to war so that a bow of steel is broken by mine arms.

LOOSED FROM BONDAGE

I **ISA 58:6** Fasting and prayer -- You bring your spirit and body under authority of your spirit, through prayer and fasting.

II In bondage. **(ISA 5:13)** (**MR 5:1-5** A prisoner of Satan) Whom Satan hath bound. No man is free who is a slave to the flesh. Devil wants to put you in bondage, corrupt, defile, contaminate us. Sin is like a soft bed, easy to get in, hard to get out. **PS 102:20** God hears the groaning of the prisoners. Different kinds of prisons: bondage and captivity. ***PR 5:22* His own iniquities shall take the wicked himself and He shall be holden with the cords of his sin. *2 TIM 2:26* That they may recover themselves out of the snare of the devil who are taken captively him at his will.** Source -- Birthing place -- origin root cause is demonic.

PS 146:5-10

III **ANOINTING**. Destroy, break, melt, set free, unbind, release, liberate). Burden removing yoke destroying power of God. Let God arise and his enemies be scattered. ***ISA 61:1*** ***Proclaim liberty to the captives.*** **LUK 4:18** Deliverance to captives. ***2 COR 3:17*** ***Now the Lord is that Spirit. Where the Spirit of the Lord is, there is liberty.*** ***ISA 10:27*** ***Destroyed because of anointing.*** ***PROV 11:9*** ***Through knowledge shall the just be delivered.*** ***JHN 8:32*** ***Ye shall know the truth and the truth shall make you free.*** ***ROM 8:2*** ***For the law of the Spirit of Life in Christ Jesus has made me from the law of sin and death.*** ***ISA 42:5-8**

MAT 16:18,19. Bind and Loose. Shall not hold out against her forbid. Bind and loose (keys). Gates of hell no prevail. ***DEUT 28:7*** ***The Lord shall cause then enemies that up against thee to be smitten before thy face, they shall come out against thee one way and flee before thee seven ways.*** **JHN 8:36** ***If the Son therefore shall make you free you shall be free indeed.*** **1 JHN 3:8** Destroy (loose)

ISA 59:19** Lift up a standard. ***I COR 4:20 ***For the kingdom of God is not in word but in power.*** ***I COR 2:5*** ***Our faith should not stand in the wisdom of men but in the power of God.*** **ECCL 8:4** Where the Word of a king is there is power. **EPH 4:8**
***EPH 4:8** He led captivity captive, (captives into captivity) prisoners.

V **FREEDOM**. No word was ever spoken that has held out greater hope, demanded greater sacrifice, ever came closer to being God's will on earth. True freedom is only found in God.

BROKEN HEARTED HEALED!

MARK 5:24-34

:24 Crowd pressed Him from all sides - almost to suffocate, **:25, 26** Condition, state, predicament = Hemorrhages, suffered, from sickness and humanity, resources gone, grew worse, {wanted to be well} Perfect picture of humanity! "NO HELP" **EPH 2:12** ** Just one of the crowd, UNTIL

:29,30 Healed of distressing ailment, By virtue **PS 30:2** ***O Lord my God; I cried unto thee, and thou hast healed me.*** **JOB 3:20** ***Wherefore is Light given to Him that is in misery and life unto the bitter in soul.*** **PS 40:13** ***Be pleased, O Lord to deliver me, O Lord make hast to help me.*** **LUKE 4:16-30**

** Can rejoice!!! But what is involved? Every blessing, benefit, provision, is an act of God's love.

LUKE 4:16-18 Spirit upon for this purpose. Six reasons. Jesus came to help the hurting, assist, came to bat for us! {Did nothing until anointed} **BROKEN HEARTED.** Shattered, downtrodden, bruised, broken in pieces, destroyed by pressure, crushed by calamity. **HEART** = Center, core, very fiber of being.

PS 147:3 ***He healeth the broken in heart and bindeth up their wounds.*** **MATT 12:20** ***A bruised reed shall he not break, and smoking flax shall he not quench.*** **LU 4:23** Spirit physician. **PS 46:1** ***God is our refuge and strength a very presenthelp in trouble..*** **ISA 40:1** ***Comfort Ye Comfort Ye my people saith your Go***d.

:25, 27 Elijah sent to widow. Elisha to Naaman. Provision and healing were available -- Only two received! Same today! Salvation, healing of hurts! Deliverance.

:28 Infuriated, enraged, why? Heathen delivered religious descendants of Abraham not.

MR 5:27,28,29 1) Heard have to hear, our part, preach 3 times in **LU 4:1 & 19, 15:8** in NT = proclaim, declare, tell. **2)** Said, kept saying what she desired. **3)** Did, pushed way through crowd, she acted out. **4)** Believed, trusted had confidence in what she heard about Jesus.

{Most believe God cares, helps, heals provides. Show God you mean business. Must not allow pain, emotions, people circumstances to stop you.

ISA 50:4 ***The Lord has given me the tongue of the learned that I should know how to speak a word in season to him that is weary.***

RELEASING THE POWER OF GOD
POINT OF CONTACT

GEN 1:1-3, ROM 12:3, MARK 5:25-30

GEN 1:1-3 Nine times (God says) Filled with faith "calls those things" Holy Spirit moved when God spoke faith. Gehazi saw. (already existed) "Every one saved at Calvary"

Faith plus Word -- Faith? 1) Link between natural and spiritual. **2)** Product of

God from heart. **3)** Its the meeting ground between limited man to limitless God.**4)** Invisible hand bring spiritual into physical. **5)** Only pleases God. **6)** Simply believing what God says -- Speaking and acting.

Holy Spirit is hovering over us. Word with Faith (Faith gives substance) **ROM 12:3** Is dealt-given and measured from God. "It isn't enough just to have faith" Has to be turned loose, use it, released.

MRK 5:25-30 **:34** Her faith released power. 1) She said 2) **:28** Image of seeing and feeling (hope) 3) Establish point of contact to release to release faith.

CONTACT -- Set action and time where you release your **FAITH**. Anything that helps you to come to a climax in your faith and release it to God.

It focuses your faith on God. (Magnifying glass) Ex: runner and a gun fire. "Its expectancy" **:28** If I may but touch His clothes.

(All power has a point at which you make contact). A car -- light switch -- Source is connected to load. Unable to release your faith without point of contact. Might be -- hands -- oil --Word of God. Ex: myself -- centurion. Set time for releasing your faith -- Turn Loose will put Holy Spirit to work. (women touch cloak -- flowed) Capacitor-horse-jet.

You reach God by establishing a point of contact, releases power.

Ex: Moses and Red, Shout & Jericho, David and Slingshot, Peter's Shadow, Samson and hair, Mary and Word, Centurion and Word, Jesus and Word, Peter and come, Simon's mother and touch, Leper and Word, palsy and act on Word, handkerchiefs and aprons.

1) Say the Word 2) See yourself free 3) Establish point of contact 4) Act on it 5) Release your faith A) Heard 6) Receive your healing **GOD'S TIME IS ALWAYS THE NOW!**

DOING THE IMPOSSIBLE

MATT 14:22-36

:22 Gave order, "HIS WILL" ex. didn't say, think about it, you feel like it, form a committee. (Obeyed, did not ask why, did not give their opinion) **:23** If going to minister to people and the impossible must get alone with GOD!

:24 **Midst** = middle of performing God's will. Tragedy strikes, storm, tempestuous adversity. **Tossed** = Agitate, tortured, vexed. **Contrary** = against, opposite, opposed, hostile. (wind & storm symbolic of Satan and circumstances) * Try to stop you from doing God's will. *Diametrically opposed to God! Black-white, cold-hot, north-south, day-night, fire-water (Didn't quit, throw in towel, turn around, but pushed on) **PHIL 3:14** I press **:25** 3 o'clock, God's supernatural presence and power came on the scene

:26 Religious, ignorant, superstitious people miss God's blessings. Of the devil -- say. (They have put God in a box) **Fear** = terror, scared, panicked. **:27** Cheer = boldness, courage, merry, "joy of the Lord in strength" **I AM -- the word spoke, killed fear --** **:28** Master (of all) must recognize before you'll respond. **:29** Come, it's up to us now! Get out, went against natural upbringing. *Entered supernatural (in Spirit all things possible) Got out and walked, not until Jesus spoke to him. Go beyond self -- "Total dependence on God" -- not self, skill, talent ability, not by power or might, but by spirit and remember the name of the Lord.

:30 Saw wind -- felt regard, take heed to, circumstances, looked at problem.

*Abraham. **ROM 4:9 & 18.** Caused Fear -- Look at Word, cause Faith
Sink. Drown, swallowed up, overwhelm, devourer **I PET 5:8**

:31 Little Faith - Falter, waver, spasmodic, on and off No good reason why to be double minded. **JAMES 1:6** **:33** Did not pat Peter on back, God sustains me just believe. **JOHN 6:21**. Immediately at shore.

CHAPTER TWO

MY GRACE IS SUFFICIENT

2 COR 12: 1-10

MAIN ISSUE: Knowledge of God! (Paul) Ever developing knowledge of God. All ways: learning! **:4** Lawful (possible) **:5** I will not glory...! Infirmities: weakness.
:7 Messenger "Angels" 188 times. Angel 181 times. Messengers: 7 times
Buffet: rap with a fist blow after blow. **2 COR 11:23-28**. Blows of Satan
Exalted: God's desire to...

I PET 5:6-7 (MATT 23:12, LUKE 14:11, 18:14) Resist the devil! God only promotes people He can trust. **:8,9** Grace: unmerited favor and ability.
Sufficient: Arkao = content and enough. [1] Raise a barrier [2] Independent [3] Self-sufficient
In weakness: realizes inability so leans on the Lord! Rest: Abide with, take up residence!

HEB 13:5&6 I will not, I will not cease to sustain and uphold you, I will not, I will not, I will not let you down! Count every trial as opportunity to prove God's Word!

GIVE I THEE!

WHERE THE SPIRIT OF THE LORD IS THERE IS LIBERTY "JESUS IS HERE"

ACTS 3:1-8. Man crying out for help "so many" "My life" Hopeless ****If God ever did it once, He will do it again.**

:5 Expecting to receive (most shopping and praying) Suppose to be a believer. **:6** Such as I have -- "Peter had something to give" wasn't pitty or sorrow, sympathy or tears, silver or gold, pleasures or riches (something man did not have anything to do with) Before give realize what you have! Many do not know a lot have just enough religion to make miserable. Satan wants to keep blind. Rule where ignorance and unbelief lives!

VISION Did not know who I was (God created-indwelt-empowered-Led) (touch you there touching God) Limitless power in us. Ex: Little old Lady -- 440 Pedal to the metal! "Freedom comes from knowing the truth" *I am and I have.

MATT 10:7&8 Receive power by faith. Jesus came to destroy works of devil.

ACTS 3:6 Name of Jesus (Not by power nor by might) **MARK 16** See yourself as God sees you.

ANOINTING IMPARTED

MR 16:9 Resurrection. Meaning. **ROM 8:11**. But if the Spirit of him that raised up Jesus **MATT 28:18.** All power is **:19** Go ye **LU 10:19** ***Behold, I give unto...*** *Impartation of new life, authority and the anointing. **:10-:11** Believed not ***2 TIM 2:13 If we believe not, yet he abideth faithful: he cannot deny himself***... **:14** Unbelief, hardness, *Ties the hands of God! **:15,:16** Believeth = Saved **(whole)** Not = damned. **:17** Believe, opens up realm of supernatural **:18** Lay hands **(impartation of healing)** **LU 4:40** ***Now when the sun was setting, all they that had any sick with divers diseases brought them unto him; and he laid his hands on everyone of them and healed them.*** *Must come into contact with the resurrected Christ, before we can impart his life. **MR 5:30.** Virtue went out of him.

ACTS 4:31-33

II **ACTS 4:31-33** Great power, witness to resurrection. **5:12** By hands: signs and wonders. Recipients of the light, glory, and power of God. *Silver and gold have I not. ***2 COR 4:7 But we have this treasure in earthen vessels, that the excellency of the power may be of God, and not of us.***

ACTS 19:6

III **ACTS 19:6**. Laid his hands **8:18** Laying on of the apostles hands Holy Ghost was given. **:11-12**. Extraordinary, powers, wonders. **DUET 34:9** Joshua the son of Nun was full of the Spirit of Wisdom for Moses had laid his hands upon him (from Paul's body, virtue, power, tangible. ***I TIM 4:14. Neglect not the gift that is in thee, which was given 2 TIM 1:6 Wherefore, I put thee to remembrance etc.***

FIFTEEN REASONS FOR MIRACLES

I **MATT 4:23-25** Healing all sickness, disease, palsy, possessed etc.

[1] Demonstrate God's will. **JHN 6:38** ***For I came down from heaven, not to do mine own will, but the will of Him that sent me... HEB 10:7 Then said, I, lo, I come to do thy will, O God.*** [2] Demonstrates God's power over Satan: ***ACTS 10:38 You know of Jesus of Nazareth who went about ....*** [3] Destroyed Satan's works. ***1 JHN 3:8 For this purpose was the Son of God ...*** [4] Prove God was with Him and us (**ACTS 10:38**) [5] Prove kingdom of God present.

II **MATT 12:28**. **I COR 4:20**. ***For the kingdom of God is not in word, but in power***.

MATT 8:16,17

III **MATT 8:16,17** [6] Demonstrates full salvation for body, soul, and spirit. Salvation is not only for the Spirit of man. [7] Give abundant life **JHN 10:10** [8] **(:17)** Fulfill prophecy [9] Confirms God's sonship, Messianic claim. **JHN 20:30,31** ..... ***But these are written that ye might believe that ye might believe that Jesus is the Christ, the Son of God: and that believing ye might have life through His name.***

[10] Glorify's God. **JHN 2:11** ***This beginning of miracles did Jesus in Cana of Galilee and manifested forth His glory and did his disciples believed on Him.*** Makes believers. ***JHN 4:48 Except ye see signs and wonders, ye will not believe.***

MRK 16:15-20

[IV] **MRK 16:15-20** [12]These signs reveal faith [13] **:20** Confirms God's word and love
[14] Sets an example for all Gospel ministers. [15] Reveals the anointing and baptism of Holy Ghost.

ACTS 1:4-8 [1] God's will [2] Power over Satan [3] Destroys Satan [4] God with us. [5] Kingdom present [6] Full salvation [7] Abundant Life [8] Fulfills prophecy [9] Son ship and ambassadors [10] Glorifies God [12] Makes believers [13] Apostles

NO FLESH SHOULD GLORY

(I COR 1:26-31, I COR 2:1-5)

JHN 15:16. Chosen and ordained us! **2:5** "Not to stand in human wisdom or philosophy" We are demonstration -- (Power and glory in the substance and life of a born again believer.) I am a miracle. You are a miracle.

1:27 All are called, but few answer the call! 3 times chosen -- selected Foolish -- dull, stupid, heedless, absurd, silly. I tried to change! "God is in business of making dead men live."**1:29** No flesh, world exalts self, we exalt God. Should glorify God everything we do. **2:2** Jesus Christ, Him Crucified "Supreme Love" Highest mountain, lowest valley, never loose its power. Demonstration of power

1:30 A) Wisdom -- If you have an ounce of brains, you will live for God. **B)** Righteousness -- ours as filthy rags rubbish *cleansed by blood "decrees in self like-esteem, confidence. **C)** Sanctification -- set apart, body in line! Walk with God will be different. **D)** Redemption -- Total freedom through cross. Possessed with God! *God needs your permission.

ORDINARY TURNED INTO EXTRAORDINARY

I COR 1:26 - **2:5** **HEB 11:6** **1:26** Few wise, mighty, noble embrace the doctrine of the cross. ***MATT 20:16* *The last shall be first, and the first last: For many be called but few chosen*.** *A chosen generation. ***JHN 15:16* *Ye have not chosen me, but I have chosen and ordained you.*** Qualifications of being used by God is not determined by the letters -- behind or before your name" On you age, color, or nationality, education! We are living miracles, rainbows, God's neon sign to world.

1:27 Chosen -- selected, picked his choice, option, decided, elected us.

(Outcasts, rejects) Foolish, not philosophers, craters, statesmen, nor men of wealth, power or influence. Foolish -- stupid absurd, silly, simpleton's in world's eyes. I was an idiot. The great heart of God pulsates with infinite love for the unlovable. Ex: Me.

Abraham -- God must love the common people, He made so many of them. Confound -- bewilder, perplex, puzzle. **ROM 1:22.** Professing themselves to be wise. They became fools.

***PS 8:2* Out of the mouth of babes and sucklings hast thou ordained praise. :28 Held in contempt, not up to snuff, below their standards.** You cannot be anything for until you are nothing. ***ROM 4:17* Things be not as though they are.** **:29** No Flesh Glory -- World exalts themselves. Believers exalts God. "Give credit where credit is due"

:30 Traditions and teachings of religion have stolen these blessed truths from the believers. We need to see beyond the misery shadows of this world, into the blessed realm of God's all sufficient kingdom.

Four things Jesus is to us in **2 COR 5:17** and in **ACTS 17:28** God has made us partakers of Himself, through Jesus. (Let God make you what he wants you to be)
Ordinary to extraordinary. Caterpillar to butterflies. Unlimited, no boundaries. **EPH 6:10** Not by might, nor by power, but by my spirit, **ZEC 4:6** saith the Lord of Host. **HEB 11:6.** My meat is to do the will of Him who sent. God **JHN 6:57** needs your permission. God needs your permission!

A POT OF OIL

2 KINGS 4:12, 2 COR 3:18, 1 SAM 28:10

I **2 KINGS 4:1** Creditor is come = thief, **JHN 10:10 Bondman** = slaves **:2 WHAT HAST THOU?** Take inventory of valuable items! Furniture? House? Talents? Education? No! Oil = anointing, new wine, Holy Ghost. Empty-uninhabited, vacant, ***HEB 12:1* Lay aside the sin.**

***EPH 4:22* That ye put off concerning the former ....** (Empty of Self) *** And everything that is not of GOD! Deep consciousness of our nothingness, no confidence in self. **:4 Thou shalt** = specific instructions (God's word tells us what to do) Ex: Elijah and Naaman, dunk seven times! Joshua, Gideon, Jehoshaphat etc:

:5 Vessels = brought, SHUT, = Obedience, (Lord what do you want). *** Obedience better then sacrifice. **Vessels** = Empty & very dry nothing. **Door closed** = personal, intimate.

She Poured = ***ISA 44:3 For I will pour water upon him that is thirsty and floods upon the dry ground. I will pour my Spirit upon thy seed, and my blessings upon they offspring. JOEL 2:28,29 I will pour my Spirit upon all flesh and your sons...*** **ACTS 2:17,18** Pour out filled with His love, joy, faith, anointing, power, presence. **:6 Oil Stayed** = Only flows to the depth of our hunger, emptiness. ** Thimbleful = Ex: Sparrow drinking from ocean, thinks he had it all.

2 COR 3:18

II **2 COR 3:18** ***1 SAM 28:10 For precept must be upon precept, precept upon precept, line upon line. MR 4:28 For the earth bringeth forth fruit of herself, first the blade, then the ear, after that full corn in the ear. PRO 4:18 But the path of the just is as the shining light, that shineth more and more unto the perfect day.*** More of His anointing, love, power, Spirit, blessings, hunger, when you come to let your desire to be simply possessed by Him!

Yielded, yielded more and more until God so possesses us, that from -- our bodies flows his virtue, anointing to a sick and dying world. *Filled with God, filled, filled, filled, and empty of self. **PRO13:24, 22:15, 23:13-14**

SPIRIT POURED OUT -- NUMBER 1

I **ACTS 2:14-21** Prophecy = shall become prophets or will speak God's word under the unction of the Holy Ghost -- drenched. **:18** Pour out = prophecy = Speak the mind, the will, the Word of God. {Ooze with Holy Ghost saturated, sapping} **ISA 10:5** And the glory of the Lord shall be revealed and all flesh will see it together. **Spirit gives supernatural enablement! 9 gifts of the Spirit: Signs, wonders, and conviction. **[Holy Ghost JHN 15, 16, 17]** Flesh = Spirit to affect every area. ***MIC 3:8 But truly I am full of power by the Spirit of the Lord.***

JOEL 2:21-28

II **JOEL 2:21-28 (ACTS 2:17-21)** Previous verse **:21** - Be glad, rejoice **:22** Fruit bearing **:23** Glad, rejoice its going to rain **:24** Full of wheat. "Overflow with Wine and Oil = anointing **:25** Restore **:26** Eat plenty **:27** Ye shall know I am in your midst **ISA 32:9-14** Reveals desolation, thorn, briers, tears, pain. **:15** until the Spirit be poured upon us from on high and the wilderness be a fruitful and the fruitful field be counted a forest! ***PRO 1:23* Behold I will pour out my spirit upon you**. **ZECH 12:10, ISA 44:3, PS 45:2, EZE 39:29**. **Question: If God has and is, why not more affected. **ACTS 10**

III **ACTS 10:34** Peter preaching to Cornelius with kinsmen and friends! **:38** How God anointed Jesus with the Holy Ghost and with power... **:44** Yet spake **:45** Poured out the gift of the Holy Ghost. **:46** Tongues and magnify God **Why? *ISA 44:3* I will pour water upon him that is thirsty and floods upon the dry ground. I will pour my Spirit upon thy seed and my blessings upon thine offspring.** " Hunger and thirst will be filled" **More! *PSALM 23:5* thou anointest my head with oil: my cup runneth over**. First: What is the cup? Second: What fills the cup? 2nd question first: Spirit, anointing, gifts, fruits, God's presence, love, joy, peace, goodness ... 1st question, is it your spirit? To some extent yes, ***JHN 7:38* out of your belly shall flow....** = gush, pour, Holy Ghost.

MR 5:25-30

IV **MR 5:25-30** Virtue gone out = anointing, Spirit **:34** Daughter thy faith {sucked, absorbed, assimilates, draws the anointing, Spirit, God's Glory, His presence} *Faith is a lightning rod! *God's eyes are roaming to an fro. Ex: Abraham, Noah, Moses, Joshua, etc. Faith drinks it in.

Faith is the substance that absorbs the Spirit of God, it is the cup our spiritual man holds and we drink from. "You have to have a cup, before you have a drink!" God pours out upon you to the degree of faith your possessed by. More faith bigger cup, more blessing.

EPH 6:16 Shield of Faith (why shield) it repels unbelief, sin, sickness, poverty. Yet draws attracts God's glory. Unbelief -- repels God's blessings, presence, anointing. [Jesus could heal only a few sick folk in his home town.] Unbelief draws, attracts, like a magnet, sin sickness, God's wrath, etc.

ANOINTED TO PREACH

LUKE 4:18 (Everyone) Because - Preach = Proclaim, declare, broadcast. Three Times, 158 in New Testament. **Gospel -- Good News, Glad Tidings**

*Jesus ministry = preach! Preach -- deliverance (Only method) "Not medicine and doctors, not by works, not with guns, no" Preaching, teaching, and then healing

Why? **ROM 10:17** Faith comes by hearing. "Sent Word and healed." Why most are not healed, won't come to hear!

LUKE 9:1. **LUKE 2&6**. Power and authority through preaching! **1 COR 1:10** "You'll show by your actions what you believe" *Perish -- I know for Lost -- But I'll include unbelieving believers. **Power of God** -- Preaching of cross. (Jesus accomplished.)

TITUS 1:3 Manifested His Word = **(1 PET 2:24, PHIL 4:19)** Through preaching. I preach to myself. Then, faith comes -- It manifests! "Preaching Opens Door for Healing" (More people get healed when hear)

HEB 4:2. Mix Word with Faith You get air by breathing, "Not enough just to believe" You get blessings by believing and acting the Gospel.

IN HIS PRESENCE

I **GEN 3:7&8**. Sinned, heard and hid from the presence of the Lord--God. {Got so caught up in their five physical senses forgot He was there all the time} **Would not sin if aware of His presence! "Acted like was not there" ***1 JHN 3:6 Whosoever abideth in Him sinneth not:*** Practice the presence of God. ***JER 5:22 Fear ye not me? Saith the Lord: Will ye not tremble at my presence, which have placed the sand for the bound of the sea by a perpetual decree, that it cannot pass it and though the waves thereof toss themselves, yet can they not prevail; though they roar, yet can they not pass over it?*** (When the cat is away, the mice will play)

II **GEN 4:16** Cain went out of the presence of the Lord. How? Went the way of the flesh, purposely out of God's will. **JONAH 1:3** Jonah fled from the presence of the Lord! **:10** Storm. It is a dangerous thing to walk out from under God's presence.

ISA 29:15

III **GEN 5:22** Enoch **6:9** Noah **17:1** Abram-walk before me. (Keep yourself before my eyes.) **24:40** Sent servant for wife for Isaac! ***EX 33:14 He said, my presence shall go with thee, I will give thee rest. PS 16:11 In thy presence is fullness of Joy***.

IV **PS 95:1&2**. Thanksgiving will make us aware of His presence **PS 100:1-5**.

JAMES 4:8 ***Draw nigh to God and He will draw nigh to you.*** ***JHN 15:4-7*** ***Abide in Him*** ***MATT 28:20*** ***Teaching them to observe all things whatsoever. I have commanded you: and, lo, I am with you always, even unto the end of the world.***

BORN AGAIN -- NUMBER 1

JHN 3:1-8

:3 Except **EPH 2:8** Many people deceived, thinking saved. Born again -- from above, new birth, regenerated, convicted, changed, and transformed. Most Christians do not have the foggiest idea what actually took place. Satan wants to keep up spiritually ignorant, illiterate and blind. Because etc. (Born again million times more then hope -- think or imagine) **EPH 3:20** A necessity -- see, understand, partake, experience. See who you are, "see yourself as God see you -- **:5** Water and Spirit.

EPH 5:26 Washes away sin, sickness, fear, disease. **PS 107:20** Being born again not of corruptible seed, but... **I PET 1:23** **JHN 1:12-13** To as many as received him, to them gave He the power.

:6 Two realms (**GEN 1:26 & 2:7**) or dimensions 1) Physical is dominated by physical *Natural man. 2) Spirit is to be dominated by Spirit & Word. *Believer **HEB 10:38** Now **ROM 1:17 GAL 3:11** *Stop trying to act like the world, when you are not of the world.

I COR 1:28 The things which are not bring to nought things that are. You, my friend, through Jesus can subdue and have dominion over your body, mind, emotions, circumstances and situations of life through the name of Jesus.

RIVERS OF LIFE

We are in the midst of a visitation of God and the Holy Ghost.

REV 21. Revelation is a Book of Now for the Body of Christ . It is our wedding march. We are the bride. God is the author of life. Earth is a proto type of heaven. Earth is clay model of heaven.

THE RIVER OF EDEN

I **JHN 7:37**, Any man thirst, **Drink!** Partake, absorb.

:38 Believe = according to our faith. Flow = flood, abound, to move or express freely, a current. Ex: Cannot see, but under surface. Rivers = a continuous flow, abundance, **Float, flow, move with, do not resist! E: standing in a stream, or on shore of ocean, tide, or waves hitting you. Will take you out into the deep! ***PS 147:18 He sendeth out his word and melteth them: He causeth His wind to blow and the waters to flow.***

II **GEN 2:8,-:10** A river. **1)** Pison = to bring increase, grow up, quicken, {cause word to become alive} **:13** **2)** Gihon = Bursting forth or anointing. Ex: Spring near Jerusalem = Soloman anointed and proclaimed king!

:14 **3)** Hiddekel = Rapid, aggressive, radical, bold, *Kingdon suffereth violence ....
4) Euphrates = fruitfulness, ***JHN 15:8 Here in is my Father gloried, that you bear much fruit***. **EX 2:3**

III **EX 2:3 HEB 11:23** by faith hid, placed into the nile! **:5-6, 10**. Moses -- came from the river! Jesus, led of Holy Ghost, out of the river. **EX 7:20**

IV **EX 7:20** Waters turned blood. ***PS 46:4 There is a river, the streams of which shall make glad the city of God, the Holy place of the tabernacle of the Most High. PS 65:9 The visitest the earth and waterest it. Thou greatly enrichest it with the river of God, which is full of water.***

BLOOD, FIRE, VAPOR OF SMOKE

Manna = What is it? (Bread of heaven) Beyond Concept, how, could, would. *To humble, proud, do good. **JOB 38-41**. God revealed. **:42** Thought he knew God! Admits did not. *Heard before, but now seen! **:6** Wherefore I abhor (despise) myself and repent in dust and ashes. (Cannot know God by mind, emotions, flesh) will have an impact. *Who am I? **MATT 16:16** Art Christ. **:17** Blessed art thou "only by the Spirit" **2 TIM 3:1** Perilous **:5** Form (similitude) of Godliness... *Heard not seen.

I **ACTS 2:1-4**. One of most awesome events in creation! **:16** That **:17** I will, upon all flesh (righteous and unrighteous) rains upon just and unjust. **:18** My Spirit (notice emphasis) Flesh profiteth. **:21** Whosoever calleth: **(Amp)** invokes, adores, worships. Saved = delivered, made whole, set free. **ACTS 4:12**. There is no other **:19** Blood, fire, vapor: Thick, whirling cloud. God has purpose, reason, plan. *Reality wrapped up in nature, types, shadows.

*This is true Christianity! God's plan for man. Way beyond! Ex: Tabernacle in wilderness. *Blood flowed in tabernacle. *Consuming fire above and in (roared, glowed, heat) Tornado of cloud, (covering in and above: Shekinah) (strange, awesome place) What like without blood, fire, vapor of smoke? (Dead formalism) = Modern Christianity. *Not talking manifestations. "Talking reality of Blood, Fire, Vapor of Smoke"

JOEL 2:16

II **JOEL 2:16**. **:23-30** Blood, fire, pillars of smoke. What would a bloodless Christianity be? Lost and undone. ***HEB 9:22 ..... without shedding of blood..... I JHN 1:7 ..... the blood of Jesus Christ hath cleansed.....*** **REV 7:14** Garments made white. ***EPH 2:13 But now in Christ Jesus.... COL 1:20 And having made peace..... ROM 5:9 Much more than, being now justified by his ....*** **ACTS 20:28** Purchased us with **LU 22:20** New testament in my **REV 12:11**. Overcame who's blood? Jesus: Lamb **JHN 10:10** Life. **Need blood** = need **THE FIRE LU 12:49**. I am come to send fire on... **EX 3:2** Fire in bush. **EX 19:18**. Lord descended on Sinai in Fire.

PS 97:1-6

III **PS 97:1-6**. **MATT 3:11** Baptize us with Holy Ghost and Fire **HEB 12:29**. Our God is a consuming fire. **ACTS 2:3** Cloven tongues **HEB 1:7** Ministries **PS 39:3**. While I was musing the fire burned. ***JER 20:9 His Word was in my heart as a burning fire.*** If need blood, fire, then vapor of smoke. **:2** Clouds (Shekinah) Told Moses **EX 19:9**. I come unto thee in a thick cloud. ***JOB 37:11 Till he weareth the thick cloud...*** **ISA 19:1**. Rideth upon a swift cloud. **PS 104:3** Clouds are his chariots. ***MATT 17:5 A bright cloud over shadowed them*** (transfigure) **I COR 10:2** All were baptized unto Moses in the cloud and in the sea! *Someone says do not need blood. We say no way! How about fire and vapor of smoke. *God's nature, essence, character. In the tabernacle. In us! Takes faith to apply! All three.

SPIRIT OF PREACH

LUKE 4:18-19

LUKE 4:16-17 (Holy Spirit) To preach (More in three years then anything else.) **Preaching, teaching, and then miracles and healings? Miracles happen when the Word is preached.

LUKE 1:17 Spirit of Elisha (to preach repentance) *More important then sign. Noah -- preacher of righteousness. Most old testament saints were!

JHN 15:26 **JHN 16:13** Give witness to Jesus. (Same job when in us) **JHN 3:34** Without measure, to preach! "**US TO**" (Holy Ghost) Stay under the fountain of Life. Ex: Old Faithful (Gyser)

ACTS 1:8 Some Spirit !!! **ACTS 2:17-18.** Prophesy (Speak form by divine inspiration) "Power of God is released through the Gospel" **1 COR 1:18-21** Word is lifeless until faith is breathed into it on your lips!

SPIRIT OF THE LORD IS UPON US TO PREACH!

THE WHY OF TONGUES

I COR 12:4-7 Three dimensions of Body

TONGUES Supernatural utterance inspired by God in an unknown tongue. It is a New Testament experience that is distinctive to this generation; and yet it has become one of the most controversial and misunderstood subjects of the Bible. (There are those who say it's done away with. **I COR 13:8-10** Ridicules. As long as on this side of heaven, it will not cease. (Those who say insignificant) **I COR 14:18** Did more than all, **14:5** wished that. Devil hates because of potentiality and power that is released through this Gift! **I COR 14** - Paul was not disclaiming but instructing.

10 MAJOR REASONS

1) MR 16:17 These signs, evidence of the presence and power of Holy Ghost (authenticates, substantiates, verifies God's presence.) **I COR 14:22** - Fire by night, cloud by day. **ACTS 2:3 & 4** -- Replaced with tongues. Proof to the World.

2) A supernatural means of communicating directly to God. An umbilical cord of divine fellowships **I COR 14:2 & 27,28** * Also, the devil does not understand, therefore cannot interfere (but in) hinder or obstruct your prayers like he did to Daniel.

3) Can pray the perfect mind and will of God **ROM 8:26 & 27.** (He who knows all things, can pray through us about things which our natural mind knows nothing about.) *Eliminated the possibility of selfishness entering into our prayers, or wrong praying which is out of line with the Word and the will of God!

4) Provides a way of praise and thanksgiving to God. **I COR 14:15 & 17**

5) Helps us to become God inside conscious, which is bound to effect the way I live. "We have a tendency of forgetting the Greater One in us."

6) Spiritual edifies us, not physical or mental. **I COR 14:4** (Enriches, cultivates, develops, improves us spiritually) *Out of your belly - a flowing stream that should never dry up.

7) ISA 28:11,12 -- rest, refreshment, from turmil, perplexity, insecurity, (tranquility, relaxation, vacation, restores, revives, renews) -- A tremendous pick-me-up

8) JUDE 20 - Charges, fortifies your faith. Stimulates, invigorates.

*One of the greatest spirtiual exercies there is.
Takes faith to pray in, believe it is accomplishing, etc. Prepares us for whatever the future holds in store for us. Gets us ready.

9) Keeps our bodies under the control of the Holy Spirt.

JAMES 3:2-4 Tongue is rudder and bridle of.

10) Teaches you how to yield yourself to God, thereby opening the door for the other gifts to flow.

"KEY TO MANIFESTATION OF GIFTS"

TRANSFERRING THE ANOINTING

ACTS 19:11-12, 2 KINGS 13:20,21, MATT 9:20 -- 2 KINGS 2:8, 13 & 14

Special miracles (extraordinary wonders) healed, devils driven out, made to go.

*From His Body! (anointing imparted into cloth) conveyed, transmitted, tangible,

material, real, perceptible. *Many kinds of power or energy. **2 KINGS 13:20,21** The virtue, power of God was still in Elisha's bones. Anointing = Capacitor - ability to absorb and contain. It communicated life to a dead body *More we die to ourselves more. **MATT 9:20-22** (**MR 6:53:56** Border) How did she know? **NUM 15:38-41** -ribbon of blue (**MATT 14:34-36**) perceived, tangible

DEUT 22:12 Fringes on the four quarters (wings) of they restore. **MAL 4:2** But unto you that fear my name shall the Son of righteousness arise with healing in His wings: **EX 25:20** Wings are a representative of God's presence, mercy, power

2 KINGS 2:8 13 & 14 Anointing of Elijah transmitted to Elisha (Lay hands on no man suddenly) *Mantle **ACTS 5:15** Shadow of Peter healed the sick ***3:1-8** As I have (not natural, emotional, financial) **Anointing** = transferable, transmit, convey, impart. *Believe you have and can **I JHN 2:27** **ACTS 10:38** **GAL 3:5** The same miracle working power that was in Jesus, is now in us! ***HAVE TO RELEASE THE ANOINTING IN YOU!***

VISITATIONS OF GOD -- NUMBER 1

I JHN 5: Some said not happen, not of God, natural cure. (Bible is Bible) **:1** Passover feast, Jesus, in Jerusalem. **:2** Sheep Gate, Bethesda = Mercy {A place of mercy} Great multitude -- afflicted, sick, hurting, diseased, (today's generation) *Do not know their sick! Waiting = hoping, begging, wishing something would happen, help, moving stirring, agitation, quickening) **Supernatural, miracles, divine happening. Not devil, demons, satanic, new age, or natural -- was a visitation from heaven. **:4** Angel -- angelic visitation, divine house call, sovereign move, God showing up. Not at 1st **GEN 3:8** and they heard the voice of the Lord walking in the garden, in the...why? Walk, visit, fellowship. Ex: Enoch, Noah, Abraham, Jacob, Joseph, Moses etc. **PS 8:4** What is man, that thou art mindful of him? and the Son of man, that thou visitest him? Season-now and then-unpredictable [cannot tell when God is going to move] Troubled stirred {God must first stir the hearts of men}

Impregnated the water with healing, virtue, tangible anointing. First step: into the move, visitation. **Angel stir, but they had to respond. **WHATSOEVER brought healing, deliverance, wholeness. Major problem: not enough for everyone. **:5** 38 years -hoping, praying **:6** Jesus = who? Immanuel -- God with us, word made flesh. Come to earth.

GAL 4:4 But when the fullness ... *Visitation of the Lord {walked through crowds did not know a visitation of God} **LU 1:78** The Dayspring from high hath visited us. Did not have to be sick any more. WILT thou = looking for those who will receive. **:7** Explains would but cannot! **:8** Rise = **LU 19:10** for the Son of Man is come to seek and to save that which is lost. **:9** Immediately. **JHN 4:14.** Step into the water and drink

LU 5:17

II **LU 5:17** Power = anointing, virtue, presence. To heal them {man with palsy} Divine Sovereign move, visitation. **MR 6:5** And he could there do no mighty work. Save that he laid his hands upon a few sick folk and healed them. [King of Kings, Author of Life, Alpha and Omega -- would not step into the water]

MUST 1) Be desperate, hungry. **2)** At right place, geographically and Spirit. **3)** Right time. **4)** Step in, by actions, confession.

ACTS 5:14

III **ACTS 5:14-16**. Healed everyone -- All four elements involved! Throughout history visitations of God. 1500 Reformation (Martin Luther) 1800 [Wesley Finney, Moody, Tailor] 1904 Welsh, Asuzo Street 1930 [Amy,Wigglesworth, Lake, Dowey]
1950 Healing 1970 Charismatic 1990 **NOW** *The water is stirring. God visiting.

Holy Ghost touching. Jesus is healing. [1] Desperate [2] Right place [3] Right time [4] Step in

WALKING ON THE WATER

MATT 14:22-33

MATT 14:24. Tossed = Torture vex contrary = against, opposite waves is daily circumstances, wind is the devil. **MATT 14:25** Walking = To trample down under foot for Jesus walking above, not below circumstances.

MATT 14:26. A lot of Christians afraid of tongues and gifts. **MATT 14:27** Cheer: Have courage boldness (daring) It is I that is setting the captives free.

***Isaiah 41:10* Fear thou not; for I am with thee: be not dismayed; for I am thy God: I will strengthen thee; yea, I will help thee; yea, I will uphold thee with the right hand of my righteous.**

MATT 14:28 Bid: Order, command Peter says is Your will then tell me, is it God's will we are healed? etc. **MATT 14:29** Come. Bible tells us so! Once you know God's will. **ACT!**

JAMES 1:22-24 Doer. Keep your eyes on the word of God. Look to Jesus the Author and Finisher of our Faith. Peter trampled under foot: the circumstances!

MATT 14:30. Saw: regard, take heed. Peter saw wind. Took eyes of Jesus and listened to devil. Then fear moves in, and Peter began to sink. When you start walking by Faith, keep your eyes on the Word and not the circumstances. Praise God, just in time Peter cried out and put his eyes back on Jesus or circumstances would have drowned him.

MATT 14:31. Get back on the Word, will receive help immediately. Little: Lacking confidence in Jesus. Wherefore: reached or entered. Peter didn't have to doubt. All you need is Faith the size of mustard seed.

JAMES 1:5 If any of you lack wisdom let him ask of God, ... JAMES 1:6-7. For he that wavereth is like a wave of the sea driven with the wind and tossed. For let not that man think that he shall receive any thing of the Lord.

MATT 14:32. Wind ceased. Slowly diminished. Resist the devil and he shall flee. Always going to be trials because we are in the world. **MATT 14:33** Overcome and it will glorify God.

ANOINTING WITHIN

I **JHN 3:7&8 Purpose** = reason, cause, end. **Manifested** = **I TIM 3:16** **Destroy** = obliterate, put an end, undo. (What works? **JHN 10:10**) **EPH 6:12** *Did succeed? **COL 2:15** Overcame **MATT 28:18** All power How? ***2 COR 10:4 Weapons of our warfare.....*** ***ANOINTING** = ***ISA 10:27 Yoke is destroyed because .... ACTS 10:38 How God anointed .....*** *The works that I do, how? Anointing.

I JHN 2:20

II **I JHN 2:20 UNCTION** = an anointing *If the same...that raised... ****LU 4:18 The spirit of the Lord*** = anointing = source, origin, essence of our success. ***I PET 4:11 If any man minister let him do it as....*** [God has provided]

I JHN 2:27

[III] **I JHN 2:27** In you (after baptized in Holy Ghost) ***ACTS 1:8 Receive power, after Holy Ghost***. Ex: Seed, **child** = awesome potential. {Man not teacher -- Holy Ghost by *anointing = five fold} Taught to abide! Intimate fellowship. *Anointings can only teach and flow to the extent you believe, obey, allow God and his word to control life.

LU 6:17-19

[IV] **LU 6:17-19** Sought = struggled. **VIRTUE** = Power, anointing, life of God -- creative ability. Ex: Lightning rod *vessel, container, capacitor [recipients of the light, glory, anointing, power of God] (16 buckets water, 1 mud) *Carry around a certain spirit! Presence Ex: James, John. Know not what spirit of Son of God came not condemn, but might have life. Ex: cup-dip in = ful of

LU 8:43-46

[V] **LU 8:43-46** Virtue flowed = power, anointing, life, light, glory *She dipped her cup into his well\out of you belly - whatever it is full of. *Anointing is received and released by what you
[I] Hear, [II] See [III] Believe [IV] Act

DIVINE POTENTIAL

EQUIPPED FOR ACTION

Jer 1:4-10 Eph 4:11-15

Jer 1:5I formed, I knew, I sanctified, I ordained, You and I. You have God's personal care. Deut. 32:10 Apple of Eye.

2 Cor 4:7 Treasure. We have infinite value and usefulness, most prized, masterpiece. Not worth any more then the next guy.

Jhn 10:10 Steal kill destroy.

:6 I cannot. {not unusual, Moses, Gideon, Heb 11 all of these} They saw themselves as useless to God, even as a hindrance. God can do more Through you then your mind could ever hope, imagine or dream of. May be It seems your not worth much in your present condition, but if you will yield your life to God, when He gets down with you will be valuable beyond description.

:7&8 Four directions:

1. Do not confess I cannot. Pull down psychological barriers.

Ps 8:2 Out of the mouth of babes and sucklings has thou ordained strength.

2. Go. Do not stay, warm the pews, sit around etc.

3. Say. Speak as God leads, open your mouth! You will

4. never find out what God has placed within you till you get in position of a demand being put on it! Example: A bird must jump before it will ever fly or find out!

5. Fear not. **2 Tim 1:7** God has not given us a Spirit of fear.

:10 Purpose: Commissioned, authorized, deputized.

:9 His hand, imparted His anointing, equipped, provided, never the same! Jesus did not purchase us with precious blood to leave us the same as he found us. *God equips, furnished, prepares, provides. We are God created, indwelt, empowered, equipped, led. {You may not realize this, but we are obligated by God's ability!}

I Cor 15:10 By the grace of God, I am what I am. God is really not asking us to do it, but let him do it through us.

Heb 11:34 Out of weakness were made strong. Plain ordinary everyday people, no bodies, changed by God into awesome vessels of glory.

I Pet 4:11 If any man minister, let him do it as the ability which God giveth.

Eph 4:11-15 Gifts. (Not nurse maiding, pampering, etc.)

3 major purposes:

1. Perfecting
2. Work
3. Edifying

To supply with the necessities in order to fulfill their particular functions. We must be equipped, prepared, trained and well-grounded for the job were called to. Must understand the divine purposes of these gifts.

Coach: Teach, instruct, educate, prepare, cultivate, develop, train, prime, urge, admonish, prompt. Bring to a place of usefulness.

Jhn 21:15-17 Feed, build, train, equip, lead. My place is to lead you to a place of action.

CHAPTER THREE

DIVINE POTENTIAL - NO 1

Jhn 3:30-31 Lu 1:52 Heb 7:7 Phil 2:5-9 Isa 57:15

Jhn 3:30-31 More self: Less God, more flesh. Less self: more God, less flesh. When your decreased, and He is increased, God's life will also increase. The more God conscious you become, the less flesh conscious you will be when He increase so will faith commitment, love so much self.

Lu 1:52 Matt 11:29, take my yoke upon you and learn of me for I am meek and lowly in hear and ye shall find rest unto your souls. God opposes those who exalt themselves above others. Jesus must be more important to you then yourself. Many are busy working for the benefit of their flesh.

Heb 7:7 Blessed of better. When we recognize our inabilities, we will become totally dependent upon His abilities. Self, love, praise, ambition, centered.

Phil 2:5-9 Jesus emptied himself to let his Father's will flow through Him, we must recognize and acknowledge we are nothing in self. Our lives must be a reflection of His desires.

Isa 57:15 Ps 10:17 Lord thou has heard the desire of the humble, thou wilt establish their heart.

Pr 24:5 You a man of knowledge increaseth strength.

MAN PLUS GOD #1

Amos 9:13 Matt 3:1-3 II Cor 9:6-7 Heb 10:35-36

Amos 9:13 Man and God makes an unbeatable team.

God is:

A. Soil

B. Seed

C. Water

Man is

1. Plow
2. Sow
3. Reap

Matt 13:3 Plow the soil (condition of soil must be just right or have a crop failure. Parable of sower is about the condition of the soil. Don't plow: Soil is hard, unproductive and ran over with words.

Mr 3:5 6:52, 8:17 People did not receive because of hardness of heart. Till cultivate the soil to break it up, which kills the weeks and prepares to receive seed. {Must plow deep, not shallow} To many. *First and hardest job, causes sweat, takes diligent active labor to plow.

Ecc 9:10 Whatsoever thy hand findeth to do, do it with all thy might. [Going to have to buckle down and make the dust fly. It will take all you have plus God]

Prov 20:4 The sluggard will not plow by reason of the cold, therefore shall He beg in Harvest and have nothing.

Prov 19:15 An idle soul shall suffer hunger.

Lu 9:62 No man, having put his hand to the plow and looking back, is fit for the kingdom of God. Have to be an extremist, fanatic, bombastic.

Matt 3:1-3 Jhn plowing the fields of mens souls and spirits. Repent: to be convicted and turn from darkness to light. Lie to Truth. Including wrong thinking, teaching, living, and speaking [Saints]

Matt 3:8 Bring forth fruit meet for repentance. Obey and do.

Hosea 10:12 Break up your fallow ground: For it is time to seek the Lord. {Only those who earnestly seek God and pay the price will reap the benefits}

GOING TO HAVE TO PLOW INTO THE WORD

SOW Deposit, to scatter or plant seed for growing a crop harvest. Farmer must sow or won't reap (cry, beg, please, bowl, no good) How much? Only reap in direct proportion of sewing [get what give]

II Cor 9:6&7 Purposeth: determine, decide, resolution.

Isa 32:20 Blessed are ye that sow beside all waters, or at all times.

Eccl 11:4 He that is observing or concentrating on the physical world doesn't sow.

Lu 4:18 Kind of seed. Jesus: life, healing, prosperity, victory, joy, faith, etc. Strange and awesome thing there is life in it dormant, hibernation. {Bible is like a bag of seeds, with God's life in them.} Born of incorruptible seed..

Gal 6:7-9 Whatsoever a man soweth that shall He also reap

Job 4:8 Even as I have seen, they that plant iniquity and sow wickedness reap the same. The one who plants the seed is held responsible for what grows [mediate].

REAP To obtain, receive, appropriate, acquire

MR 11:24 Reveals that you receive by Faith

Heb 10:35-36 Ye might receive the promise

Gal 6:9 And let us not be weary in well doing: For in due season we shall reap if we faint not.

Heb 6:12 Be not slothful, but followers of them who through faith and patience inherit the promises.

PLOW - PLANT - GOD GIVES INCREASE = REAP

MAN PLUS GOD #2

Amos 9:13-15 1 Cor 3:6-9 Isa 54:2&3

Amos 9:13 Supernatural acceleration, instantaneous growth.

Man plowing and sowing seeds: Soon as hit the ground immediately vine would grow and grapes would form, ripened, and mature then picked by a treader! {That is fast honey -- productivity to the limit; supernatural acceleration} *Day's=Now (talking about the body of Christ)

Dan 4:4 Many shall run to and fro and knowledge shall be increased.

I Cor 3:6&9 God caused that which was sown to grow and produce

Ps 115:14 The Lord shall increase you more and more.

Isa 40:29 Them that have no strength He increaseth strength

Isa 60:22A little one shall become a thousand and a small one a strong nation. I the Lord will hasten it in His time.

Jer 1:12I hasten my word to perform it.

Very important over riding fact: Miracles do not just happen. Takes man cooperating with God to accomplish the impossible.

Matt 14:15-21 Five loaves and two fish

{Going to take all you have and God}

Isa 54:2&5 Commands and requirements.

Enlarge, stretch forth, lengthens and strengthen.

Phil 3:14I press toward the mark [Exert yourself]

(Must have and eager, intense desire and determination to move on with God)

Rev 3:16 Luke warm complacent, idle, inactive, smug, dead head {stay frisky, energetic, ferverent} Hot, boiling, glowing, burning desire for God's will to.

James 5:16 Fervent prayer of a righteous man availeth much!

Col 1:10 Being fruitful in every good work and increasing in knowledge of God.

DIVINE POTENTIAL NO 2

RELEASING HIS POTENTIAL!

AND TAPPING INTO HIS ABILITY!

I Sam 10 5&6 Isa 16:22,23 II Kings 3:11 & 15,16 Isa 40:31 Eph 5:17-21

I Sam 10:5,6 Turned into another man. When the Spirit of God comes on you and your yielded, you will never be the same. (Musical instruments)

16:22,23 Saul refreshed well, foil, Spirit left.

II Kings 3:11 :14-20 Hand of the Lord came upon Him. He composed himself to receive instructions from God.

Isa 40:31 They that wait minister and stir themselves up.

Eph 5:17-21 Filled: Controlled speaking to self = personal application. Psalms, hymns, Spirit songs. (In your heart)

:20 Giving thanks.

:21 Submitting, humility

Col 3:16 Let the Word of Christ dwell in you richly in all wisdom; teaching and admonishing one another in psalms and hymns and spiritual songs, singing with grace in your hearts to the Lord.

Stir yourself up for spiritual comes to surface.

Mr 14:3-9 She broke the box to release what was within it. Notice it says the ointment of spikenard was very precious not the box. We give so much time to that which will perish and so little to that which will go on throughout eternity.

It the inner life, not the flesh that is so valuable to God. I want you to recognize the value of your inner man. Or you won't give it the time and attention it needs. The most valuable thing about you is your inner man. Best investment is Spirit. Flesh is vanity. You in your inner man.

Isa 62:3 Thou shalt also be a crown of glory in the hand of the Lord and a royal diadem in the hand of thy God.

It is the inner life that has a spiritual fragrance that is so beautiful.

Jhn 12:5 And the house was filled with the odor of the ointment. Heavenly aroma, Godly fragrance, Divine incense we need to fumigate the world with the presence of god. (We are to be a breath of life) God himself generates a divine fragrance.

Song of Solomon 2:1 I AM the rose of Sharon and the lily of the valleys.

Eph 5:2 Jesus gave Himself for us an offering and a sacrifice to God for sweet smelling savor. How do we smell, when its the flesh it stinks: thinking, attitude, disposition. Language and the way we act. (reek selfishness)

Jer 8:18-22 Poured out. Balm of Gilliead. A precious costly ointment that was kept in a sealed container, which must be broke open to release its precious contents. Then poured into the wounds. Jesus poured himself into the hurts of humanity. Pour ourselves into humanity. Song: I will be poured out like oil upon the alter for you. Jesus poured himself into us, for we could pour ourselves out to others. Jesus poured out His life, Zohe, God's life, must let the Life of God pour out of us, not the life of the flesh.

Broke: There had to be a breaking of the box before could be a release of the inner ointment. Site had to break.

I Cor 11:24 This is my body broken for you.

Eph 2:14 Wall of partician broken. Broken: to loosen, especially by way of deliverance.

Must be a destroying of the strong will of the flesh. Flesh is weak.

Lu 10:9 Healeth sick that are there in. There must be a release of the Spirit of God in order to attract, convict, and enlighten sinners.

Mat 21:47 **Lu 20:18** whosoever shall fall upon that stone shall be broken: but on whomsoever it shall fall, it will grind him to powder.

DIVINE POTENTIAL NO. 3

SIN NO MORE

JHN 8:1-11

:4 Taken in sin. All of us have been caught red handed, unquestionably guilty. (Spiritually, emotionally, hurting sick)

:5 Stone by Moses law (wanted to hang her high -- no mercy) Condemn her to death. Why? She did not have any value or worth to them, she was dispose able, *Natural man judges worth of a person upon their own opinions, but we need to see the worth of a person upon the scale that God has established. What worth have you placed on a human soul. *How we treat people reveals the value they have to us.

:6 Accuse looking for something in order to teardown, belittle, criticize. Satan is accuser, **I Pet 5:8**, seeking whom he may devour. **Mal 3:11** -- Devourer condemns.

Heard them not. Close your ears.

Matt 27:12 Answered nothing. :14 Not a word.

:7 Cast stone if without sin (Could have said yeah, your right, stone her) Why didn't? Jesus saw her as valuable. Did not look at her through the eyes of the flesh. *Did not see as was but could be! Valued the possibilities of the human soul, more than He did His own life. Jesus believed in her, had hope for her -- invested in her. Do we value the worth of a human soul more than we value our own lives. Pride and reputation.

Generation after generation has gone to hell, while the church waits for God to do something.

:10&11 Neither do I condemn.

Jhn 3:17 For God sent not his Son into the world to condemn the world but that the world through him might be saved.

Sin no more. That is what God is saying. He does not condone sin.

Isa 55:7 Let the wicked forsake his way and the unrighteous man His thoughts and let him return unto the Lord, and He will have mercy upon him and to our God, for he will abundantly pardon. If we are in step with the world we are out of step with God.

Jhn 16:14 Forsake. Let not sin dwell no more, lest a worse thing come unto thee.

Job 11:14 If iniquity be in thy hand, put it far away and let not wickedness dwell in thy tabernacle.

I Pet 4:17 For the time is come that judgment.

Jhn 15:2 That it may bring forth more fruit. Cannot expect sinner to repent if Christians won't. You would not give me a dirty plate to eat from.

Rev 3:19 As many as I love, I rebuke and chasten be zealous therefore, and repent.

Jhn 15:2 That is it may bring forth more fruit. God of another chance. (I wouldn't give you a dirty glass.)

DIVINE POTENTIAL NO 4

STIRRED UP

Deut 32:10-13 Apple of His Eye, :11 stirreth -- pushes the eaglets out the nest, watches over, and comes to their rescue. God wants to get out of the nest, (on the job training) You may understand God's principles in theory but must know by experience.

Jude 16:19,20 Delilah: Symbolic of satanic devices the devil uses us to drain our spiritual strength.

I Pet 2:11 Dearly beloved, I beseech you as strangers and pilgrims, abstain from fleshly lusts, which war against the soul.

:20 As at other times shake myself other times, lion, slayed thirty philistines, killed 1,000, carried away the gate problems, that became opportunities, challenges. Every problem can be used as an opportunity to draw on the life of God within you. (If there was never an impossible situation, never would need a release of divine potential) Example: Absolute desperate, adrenaline. {spiritual adrenaline} But first must be a demand put on you. Shake himself. Hebrew Word: the rustling of the lions mane which usually accompanies the lions roar. He shook stirred, fired, worked himself up. "Then there would be a release of the anointing"! We must shake ourselves up. To do, to be, to reach out in the new year.

Isa 64:7 Stirreth up himself to take hold. Shake yourself, awaken, arouse yourself spiritually. If you sit back and do nothing that exactly what is going to happen.

2 Tim 3:7 Ever learning, never able to come to the knowledge of the truth. When you know the truth and the truth shall make you free.

I Cor 15:34 Awake to righteousness and sin not for some have not the knowledge of God; I speak this to your shame.

2 Tim 1:5,6 That thou stir up the gift of God. Stir: to awake, arouse, kindle a fresh, keep in full flame, for the flame, fire yourself up.

There must be a release of the Spirit of God in order to attract, convict, enlighten sinners. We must make up for lost time, men and women of action, live wires, spiritual dynamos, aggressive, yet up and get!

DIVINE POTENTIAL NO 5

HIS TALENTS

Matt 25:14-30

:14&15 His goods, talents

II Cor 4:7 But we have this treasure in earthen vessels, that the excellency of the power may be of God and not of us. God does not see us as we are, but can be! Examples: Gen 17:5 Abram--Abraham. :15 Sarai--Sarah

Gen 32:28 Jacob--Israel.

Rev 3:12 Him that overcometh, a new name is given. Jesus did not purchase us with His blood to keep us the same but to change us into a new person. Gave them His talents to do a job, commissioned us, ordained to bring forth fruit. We are obligated by God to reach out to others.

:16&17 To Doers: **Rev 12:11** ... and they loved not their lives unto death. A man is no fool who gives what He cannot keep. To gain what He cannot loose. A pure heart is when a person is not afraid to accept the responsibility that God has placed within His hands and sets out to do it!

:18 In the earth, he buried himself into this world, talents, money, energy. (Buried in earth ungodly side springs up. You will never find out what God has placed within you till you let God put a demand on it. Example: Like a baby bird. My son, Steven afraid of falling.

Many live their whole lives never realizing their true God given potential undiscovered potential is like undiscovered gold.

Plant yourself in God, you will grow like a cedar in Lebanon, palm tree.

:23 **Heb 11:6** He that cometh to God, must believe that He is giving your best to God is an opportunity you won't want to pass up.

:25 Excusing away their obligation to work (I am not good enough.

:26 God made an investment to get a return. Entrusted us.

:29 **I Cor 15:34**, Awake to righteousness and sin not. For some have not the knowledge of God. I speak this to your shame.

GOD GIVEN

ABILITY GOD GIVETH NO. 1

I PETER 4:10-11

Ability: To exercise force, to have power! Grace: God's unmerited ability. Imagine the infinite power of God, with that awesome power the planners and stars were created. The earth was formed and man was brought forth upon it!

Same limitless power is looked up in your inner man, waiting to be released! You have God's ability in you just waiting for it to mainfest.

Our worst enemy is our self. We limit God, or allow to be limitless in us!

Zec 4:6 Not by might, nor by power, but by my Spirit, saith the Lord! If you choose to face life by yourself, God will let you go it above. He respects your freedom to decide your own spiritual destiny. (Flesh won't do job) Christianity: Supernatural walk, supernatural way of life.

I Cor 2:1-5:4 :5 Depended on God, Period! Paul: no confidence in flesh! "Had education university of Tarsus." *Workers.

2 Cor 6:1 **Vain**. The presense of God's awesome power does you little good if you do not allow that power to work in and through you. A lot never relase God's ability? Are you too lazy to seek God.

ONE DAY AT A TIME

THE GOD GIVEN ABILITY NO. 2

I Pet 4:10-11 2 Pe 1:2-3 Eph 6:10 I Cor 15:10 2 Pe 3:18

I Pe 4:10-11 Minister. Serve, wait upon. Ability. Have or exercise force. Not our ability. Respond to His ability. "Let Him do it through you" (God created, indwelt, empowered, led) Same miracle working power manifested in Jesus imparted in us. "Not by power nor might but by my Spirit, God".

II Pe 1:2-3 Grace is unmerited ability. God abounding. Knowledge not information (spare tire) I AM, I HAVE, I CAN.

Eph 6:10 In Lord, "Won't get ahead leaving GOD behind." You only conquer life to the extent that you contact God (See self as God sees)

Psychological barriers. Example: Elephant. God wants us to soar like eagles, but many Christians are content to scratch like chickens. Devil knows you can, so says He you cannot.

I Cor 15:10 Yet not I. Die to Self like, esteem, confidence, for Jesus to increase. Kingdom not built on leftovers. Consuming fire, clothed in power. Only flow to extent of Word in Life.

2 Pe 3:18 Grow. Enlarge, increase amplify.

Stop wrestling with the Word of God and start resting. Ever going to accomplish anything. Have to be in God's ability.

THE GOD GIVEN ABILITY NO. 3

1 Peter 4:10-11

:10 "Every man". Minister: Serve, wait upon! One to another. World put's itself first. We put God first and our selves last.

:11 In God's ability, to have or exercise force! Not your ability, why so many never do anything. Realize already have God's ability and that you do not have to be a big shot to set free. Why? Found out step out in faith. Example: Peter on water. "God's ability" People struggle.

2 Peter 1:2-3 Grace: Gods unmerited ability. His-has (ability) All things (repeat) Doesn't want us to know. Do not pray something you have! Admit: I have what the Bible says I have and I am etc. "All Jesus is and did is ours."

Eph 6:10 In the Lord, not self. You decide. You can "devil" knows you can so he says you can't. See yourself as God see you! Refuse to see anything else.

Luke 9:61&62 Looking back. Past life, faults, inabilities, weaknesses. Old man gone. New creation! New species of man. For your information: effective. World: Be reasonable and sensible. No lets be Bible. We are God created, God indwelt, God impowered, and God led.

ONE WAY, ONE JOB; JESUS AND SOUL WINNING!

THE GOD GIVEN ABILITY NO. 4

I Peter 4:10-11

I Peter 4:10-11 — **Ability**. To have or exercise force. Grace: God's unmerited favor and ability. "I am what God's word says I am" God created, indwelt, empowered, led. See yourself as God sees you.

Gift. Special spiritual enablements! God given abilities. It is God who is at work in you. The devil knows you can, so he say's you cannot.

I Cor 15:9-10 — I AM what I AM "Moses, Joshua, David, Jonathan, Samson, Elijah, etc. The miracle working power that was manifested in Jesus, is now imparted in us. Not in vain and not useless. I cannot do anything. But I know some one who can through me.

Eph 3: 7-8 — Paul ministered in God's ability!

I Peter 5:5-7 — Proud. God gives grace to the humble. Thinks or tries to do it in himself! Humble: "Esteeming yourself small in as much as we are so, and therefore being completely dependent on God and receiving all we need from HIM."

Christian suffer today because they try to do it on their own.

2 Peter 3:10 — **Grow**. Enlarge, increase, amplify. Grace and knowledge is God. It flows from God through us.

THE GOD GIVEN ABILITY NO. 5

I Peter 4:10-11 Zec 4:6

Realize God is not asking you to do His works but let Him do them through you.

See only what He say's -- will put you over every time! "Renewing mind" Example: Psychological barriers: Elephants, pest, (new way of life) natural man cannot. (Mind of devil) You can through Jesus!

John 1:14-17 Jesus is full of grace and truth. Word and God's ability. You conquer life to the extent that you have contact with God.

:16 Fullness we received! (Yours, use it) Example: Brains, use them. "Grace for Grace"

:17 By Jesus Christ and Him crucified! "To fulfill Law" People give up to easily and become lazy. Learning to lean.

Act 4:33 Great grace? Only manifested when act on God's Word in faith. Do not settle for less. I do not want to just possess faith. Faith possesses me. Jesus = Jesus.

I Tim 1:12 Faithful to use God's ability. No one is predestined for defeat or failure. Place your life in to the hands of God. Do not have faith in yourself or man but in God.

Dan 11:32 Shall be strong and do exploits.

THE GOD GIVEN ABILITY NO. 6

I Peter 4:10-11

When we stop, Jesus will start!
God's given us His ability. (God created indwelt, empowered, led) Glorified. Only God! No way can brag.

2 Cor 3:5,6 Think anything of selves! Your not sufficient. Our sufficiency is God! Period. What we are and have is in Christ. Spirit giveth life. Not by might nor by power, but by my Spirit says Lord of Host. Flesh profits nothing.

Gal 3:1-5 Made perfect by flesh? No! Ability flows by faith.

I Cor 4,7 We must decrease in self-like, self esteem, self-confidence, for Jesus to increase! God only promotes people He can trust.

I Cor 15:10 By the grace of God I AM what I AM.

ALL THE GLORY GO'S TO GOD.

Ever going to accomplish anything it is going to have to be in God's ability.

THE GOD GIVEN ABILITY NO. 7

I Pet 4:10-11 Flows from God through us to mankind. Ability: To have or exercise force. Grace is God's unmerited ability.

:10 Every move. Get eyes off of self. Trust in Lord.

I'll speak; major key releasing God's ability. Must hear to manifest. Words of mouth fruits of thoughts.

Let God created indwelt, empowered, and led. Limitless, locked up inside. Devil knows we can so he says you cannot. I AM because God am (see yourself as God sees) Limit God or Limitless?

II Tim 2:20-21 **Vessel**: Instrument, tool, and equipment. Certain job. Purge: Clears, purify, remove impurity's or contamination. Mind number 1 area Christians defeated in. Things: iniquity. Anything that is not of Faith!

Himself -- God will not purge you, He will help you. Your decision.

Sanctify -- Set apart, yielded to God for purpose of fulfilling His will on face of earth.

Meet -- appropriate, suitable

Prepared -- Ready, available

II Tim 3:16&17 The ability of God can only flow in my life to the extent that you allow God's word to control your life. Example: Kite

ENABLEMENTS

A PREPARED PLACE

John 14: 1-6, Lu 17:20-21, Col 1:13, I John 4:17

Troubled-distressed, disquieted, upset, worry, afflicted, pain, tormented.

John 14: 1-6 Mansions: dwelling, abiding, resting. Place: joy, peace, love, victory, freedom, success. Jesus said "I Go" to cross, hell, and heaven. Prepare: Provide, make ready, arrange. **I Tim 3:16 :4** destination.

:6 Place is with the Father. Sin had separated us and Jesus reinstated us.

Heb 4:16 Throne

Rom 8:15 Abba Father (crucified, buried, hell, raised, and conquered the enemy)

Eph 1:19-22 2:6 Phil 2:9-11 Not place but position, rank, status, GO

Lu 17:20-21 Our Father prayer -- "God heard" Also- Likewise.

Col 1:13 **I Jhn 4:17** as He is so are we. Rescued us out, dominion, tyranny, control. We are in His Kingdom. Translated= Exchanged, removed, re-established, transplanted. We are only as rich and free as we see ourselves.

1 Cor 2:9 But as it is written, eye has not seen nor ear heard, neither have entered into the heart. Translated: exchange. He became one with us in death. "That we might be one with Him in life."

I Jhn 4:17 As He is so are we!

You are Satan's master today, just as Jesus when He arose.

Jhn 14:6 Way! Read, path, (manner, method, practice)
Crucified to resurrect! Matt 16:24-25 Gal 2:20

GOD WANTS TO REVEAL HIMSELF TO YOU, THROUGH YOU, AND IN YOU!

EVERYTHING WE ARE AND HAVE IS IN CHRIST JESUS.

1 COR 4:8 Now you are full, now you are rich, you have reigned as kings without us. **Rev. 5:10**. He has made us unto our God, Kings and Priests and we shall reign on the earth.

BY HIS GRACE

I **ROM 3:15:21** Addicted, hooked, main liner, {need God} **GAL 3:19** wherefore then serveth the law -- **:24** schoolmaster ...

1 COR 1:18

II **I COR 1:18** Foolishness = folly **Saved** = pathway of salvation **:20**, disputer = subtle debater **:21** Wisdom knew not = never find God through human brilliance **:22** **Greeks** = philosophy **:23** foolishness = sheer nonsense --**:25** weakness = that springs from God surpasses human strength **:26** flesh = human standard .**:27** weak = weaklings. **:28** Base = lowborn and contemptible, poor and insignificant. **JAM 2:5** Hearken my beloved.... [scrapping bottom of barrel] **:29** no flesh glory. **PRO 3:34** he giveth grace to the lowly ***I COR 2:24*** ***and my speech and my preaching was not with enticing ...*** *Tap into, move, flow, cooperate, yield, surrender, trust, rely, depend upon God. ***ZECH 10:5*** ***They shall be as mighty men, which tread down their enemies in the mire of the streets, in the battle and they shall fight, because the Lord is with them.*** **:30-31** ***I PET 4:10,11*** ***If any man minister....***

I COR 3:6-11

III **I COR 3:6** God gave = caused the growth **:7** anything = deserves credit Increase = growth **:10** grace **EPH 4:7** But unto everyone of us... = **:11** Foundation, Jesus Christ

I COR 4:5

IV **I COR 4:5 Manifest** = expose, reveal. ***EPH 5:13 But all things that are...*** **PRAISE** -- ***GAL 6:4 Let every man prove His....*** **:6 Puffed** = stop boasting not be arrogant champions. **:7** differ = superior. Why dost had achieved yourself --**:13 JAM 4:6** But he giveth more grace... **:10** humble yourself in the sight..... ***2 TIM 2:1 Thou therefore, my son, be strong in the grace that is in Christ Jesus. PS 46:1 God is our refuge and strength, a very present help in trouble.***

2 PET 1:2-4

V **2 PET 1:2-4** Grace and peace, multiplied. ***ROM 5:20 Where sin abounded, grace did much more abound. 2 PET 3:18 But grow in grace, and in the knowledge of our Lord and Savior Jesus Christ.***

I PET 4:6 Live according to God in the spirit. ***LU 2:40 & the child grew, and waxed strong in spirit, filled with wisdom and the grace of God was upon him.***

PS 84:11 For the Lord God is a son and shield: the Lord giveth grace and glory, no good thing will he withhold from them that walk uprightly.

CHAPTER FOUR

HOPE, INHERITANCE, POWER

Eph 1:15-19
Give Unto = Cause to Flow

:17 Father in Jesus Name. Abound and increase yet more and more. Personal full knowledge of Jesus.

*Rev = The revealing of God Himself in essence, character and nature.

:18 Heart -- illuminated. The very care of your being. (Christians are blind in many areas.) Color blind, near sighted, far sighted, night blindness.

:18 Hope of His Calling = confidence of His invitation. *Occupation. Example come and get it!

2 Peter 1:3&4 According as His divine power.

Heb 3:1 We are Partakers of Jesus' calling.

Best example -- Luke 4:18 destroy works of the devil. Set captives free. *Vision (People do not know it)

Phil 3:13&14 I press toward (You have to reach out)

Rom 8:17 Inheritance. We are heir and joint
Col 3:19 Says receive Abraham

Eph 1:3 "Blessed us" God's blessings are already ours

2 Pet 1:3&4 Blessings (People do not know it)

Eternal life, righteousness, better covenant, health, fruits of Spirits. All of God's Assets. God's blessings.

IF KNOW IT IN HEART, WILL ACT ON IT.

Heb 6:12 Through Faith and patience inherit the Promises.

FAITH DOESN'T DELIVER US -- JESUS DOES!!!
FAITH IS JUST THE HAND!!

:19 Power: Super eminent magnitude of His Power.

Matt 28:18 Jesus said all power has been given unto me.

Phil 2:9-11 We have Name of Jesus. *Authority -- power and ability.

Eph 6:10 Says finally, my brethren, be strong, in the Lord, and in the Power of His might.

NAME OF JESUS Hope, Inheritance, Power

EVERYTHING WE ARE AND HAVE IS IN CHRIST JESUS

I AM

1. A child of God. **(ROM 8:16)**
2. Redeemed from the hand of the enemy. **(PS 107:2)**
3. Forgiven. **(COL 1:13,14)**

4. Saved by Grace through Faith. **(EPH 2:8)**
5. Justified. **(ROM 5:1)**
6. Sanctified. **(I COR 6:11)**
7. A New Creature. **(2 COR 5:17)**
8. Partaker of His Divine Nature. **(2 PET 1:4)**
9. Redeemed from the Curse of the Law. **(GAL 3:13)**
10. Delivered from the powers of darkness. **(COL 1:13)**
11. Led by the Spirit of God. **(ROM 8:14)**
12. A Son of God. **(ROM 8:14)**
13. Kept in safety wherever I go. **(PS 91:11)**
14. Getting all my needs met by Jesus. **(PHIL 4:19)**
15. Casting all my cares on Jesus. **(I PET 5:7)**
16. Strong in the Lord and in the Power of His Might. **(EPH 6:10)**
17. Doing all things through Christ who strengthens me. **(PHIL 4:13)**
18. An heir of God and a joint heir with Jesus. **(ROM 8:17)** .
19. Heir to the blessings of Abraham. **(GAL 3:13,14)**
20. Observing and doing the Lord's commandments. **(DEUT 28:12)**
21. Blessed coming in and going out. **(DEUT 28:6)**
22. An inheritor of eternal life. **(I JHN 5:11&12)**
23. Blessed with all spiritual blessings. **(EPH 1:3)**
24. **HEALED BY HIS STRIPES (I PET 2:24)**
25. Exercising my authority over the enemy. **(LUKE 10:19)**

26. Above only and not beneath. **(DEUT 28:13)**

27. More than a conqueror **(ROM 8:37)**

28. Establishing God's Word here on earth. **(MATT 16:19)**

29. An overcomer by the Blood of the Lamb and Word of my Testimony. **(REV 12:11)**

30. Daily overcoming the devil. **(I JHN 4:4)**

31. Not moved by what I see. **(2COR 4:18)**

32. Walking by faith and not by sight. **(2 COR 5:7)**

33. Casting down vain imaginations. **(2 COR 10:4&5)**

34. Bringing every thought into captivity. **(2 COR 10:5)**

35. Being transformed by a renewed mind. **(ROM 12:1&2)**

36. A laborer together with God. **(I COR 3:9)**

37. The righteousness of God in Christ. **(2 COR 5:21)**

38. An imitator of Jesus. **(EPHESIANS 5:1)**

39. The Light of the World. **(MATT 5:14)**

WE ARE OVERCOMERS

John 16:32-33 Jesus said he had overcome the world. Doer: full of courage, confidence. Overcome: Subdue, conquer, get the victory. Victorious. (Sin, fear, sickness, pain, Satan, poverty, death)

What Jesus has done.
What he is doing.
Who we are in him.

We have to be an overcomer, (in order to ... Promises made to overcomers.)

Rev 2,7 To him that overcometh will I give to eat of the tree of Life.

2:11 He that overcometh shall not be hurt of the second death.

21:7 He that overcometh shall inherit all things, and I will be his God and he shall be my son.
Rev 2:17, 2:26, 3:62, 3:21

3:5 Lets look at it.

Rom 8: 35-37 Some Christians believe verse 36 more than 37. Nay--no Conquerors as overcomers gain a surpassing victory, preeminently.

II Cor 5:17 We are new.

I John 5:4-5
4:4 Natural to overcome. Our faith in Jesus.

Rev 12:11 They overcame by the blood and word.

THE REBIRTH OF MAN #1

John 3: 1-8 Born of Flesh = Carnality and conceived in sin.Verily Verily -- With all the earnestness I possess I tell you this you must be born again. Spiritual rebirth, recreated, resurrected, remaking, reviving.

Gen 1:27 So God created man in his own image, (replica, reproduction, copy mirror), in the image of God created he him; male and female created he them.

Gen 3:7 Eyes opened, knew naked. (Died)

Eph 2:5 Were dead in our sins. Died to God. Love, divine nature, perfect health, environment, peace, joy, health, vision, purpose, plan, dreams, ideas, desires.

Matt 8:22 Dead bury the dead.

Eph 2:1 Dead in trespasses and sin.

Col 2:13 And you being dead in your sins and the uncircumcision of your flesh. Man's sin opened pandora's box. Gave birth to hate, lust, adultery, etc. (Amp Gal. 5) Fornication, uncleanness, impurity, indecency, idolatry, witchcraft, strife, jealousy, hatred, sorcery, envy, anger, selfish ambition, murder, drunkenness, carousing.

Jhn 11:25 I am the resurrection etc.

Job 19:25 For I know that my redeemer liveth, and that he shall stand at the latter day upon the earth. Resurrection: A person, Jesus, is life in its total essence life out of death. Resurrection: arouse from the sleep of death, recall dead to life. Coming back into practice. Restoration: A return to life the way it should be.

THE REBIRTH OF MAN #2

Jhn 12:24-25 Into ground and die. Single grain, kernel: produces much grain rich yield, good harvet. He was seed planted to produce bring replication of himself, duplication.

1 Pet 1:23 Being born again, not of corruptible seed, but of incorruptible, by the word of God, which liveth and abideth forever. He was the seed planted to produce more like him. A xerox copy. A replication, a reproduction, duplication, reflection, a single grain kernel which produces much grain, rich yield, good harvest. For 4,000 years the nature of God had been dead in the heart of men, now raised to life.

Matt 28:18 And Jesus came and spoke to them, saying, all authority is given to me in heaven and upon earth.

Eph 2:6 Has raised us up together and made us sit together in heavenly places in Christ. All that God is, is at our disposal.

Rom 8:11 Dwell--taken possession of you, make alive your death doomed bodies, dwelleth taken possession of you.

Eph 2:10 For we are His workmanship, handiwork, created in Christ Jesus to good works, which God has before ordained (predestined) that we should walk in them. (Daily way of Life) There needs to be a resurrection of Godliness, forgiveness, righteousness, holiness, commitment, etc. The Life that flowed through Jesus, now flows through us. Living personifications of the Life of God. Love, joy, peace, longsuffering, gentleness, etc.

Live on the resurrected side of the tomb in newness of Life goodness, faith, kindness, meekness, self-restraint, self-control etc. Give outward expression to inward reality.

Living personifications of the resurrection of Jesus. God's total personality once again taking on flesh and blood in recreated man. Recycle paper, cast more, salvage, recover, redeemed, rescued, restored, saved. Let the resurrection of God shine forth.

BORN AGAIN NO. 1

JOHN 3:1-8

:3 Except **Eph 2:8** Many people deceived, thinking saved. Born again -- from above, new birth, regenerated, convicted, changed, and transformed.

Most Christians do not have the foggiest idea what actually took place. Satan wants to keep up spiritually ignorant, illiterate and blind. Because etc. (Born again million times more then hope -- think or imagine)

Eph 3:20 A necessity -- see, understand, partake, experience. See who you are, "see yourself as God see you --

:5 Water and Spirit.

Eph 5:26 Washes away sin, sickness, fear, disease.

Ps 107:20 Being born again not of corruptible seed, but...
I Pet 1:23

John 1:12-13 To as many as received him, to them gave He the power.

:6 Two realms (Gen 1:26 & 2:7) or dimensions

1) Physical is dominated by physical *Natural man.

2)Spirit is to be dominated by Spirit & Word. *Believer **Heb 10:38** Now **Rom 1:17 Gal 3:11** *Stop trying to act like the world, when you are not of the world.

I Cor 1:28 The things which are not bring to nought things that are. You, my friend, through Jesus can subdue and have dominion over your body, mind, emotions, circumstances and situations of life through the name of Jesus.

BORN AGAIN NO. 2

II Cor 5:17 - IN -

II Cor 1:20 For all the promises of God in him.

John 15:7 If ye abide in me. Creation: species, category, class type. **Partakers of God! *God created, indwelt, empowered, led. Heavenly people, origin, citizenship, destiny, that are to live heavenly lives in a sin, sick, messed up world.

BEHOLD, look, observe, consider. (The Word - in a new world. That operates on new principals.

I Cor 3:1-4 Living like mere ordinary run of the mill men -- When in reality the sons and daughters of God Almighty. Ordinary men controlled by mind and body. Prisoner, slaves, and puppets. Walk up and realize who, have, can do in Christ. See yourself as God does.

Acts 17:28 For in Him we live, and move, and have our being (new creation receives all that he is and has from God.

Eph 5:1 Imitators. Copy, follow His example. (Reveal himself to, in and through) Living personifications, reflections. (Christian) World looks at us, should see God. Indubitable evidence. Not just here to be happy and successful but to glorify God. Be one in thought, word and action (all God is, has, ever will be at our disposal, available to us).

Col 3:10 Put on, renewed = developed, molded, shaped. *In knowledge, have to learn who you are before you can act like who you are. Your true identity is revealed in God's Word.

Rom 8:19 All of Creation is in travail. Waiting for the man. Start to act, talk and think like who you really are.

Take your rightful position (reflection of God himself to the human race).

MADE TO REIGN

Matt 14:25-29 Heb 2:6&7 Gen 22:16-18 Dan 7:27 Mrk 13:34-37

Matt 14:25-29 Peter stepped into the realm of Divine authority when He stepped out of the beat. You and I can step from the realm of flesh into the realm of the Spirit. The Word (Jesus) was more real to Him then the wind, storm and all natural elements. In that moment, He was one with God, in rhythm, symphony, harmony. "You are the Christ."

Heb 2:6&7&8 Acts 17:28 For in Him we live and move and have our being.

Matt 16:18&19 And I say also vote thee, that thou are Peter and upon this rock [:16 The Christ] I will build my church and the gates of hell shall not prevail against it and I will give unto they the keys of the kingdom of heaven; and whatsoever thou shall bind on earth shall etc...

I Cor 4:8 Now ye are full, now you are rich, you have reigned as Kings without us: and I would to God ye did reign with Him.

Rev 22:5 We shall reign forever and ever.

Gen 22:16&18 Because thou hast obeyed. Coin stamped with image.

Gen 1:27, Dan 7:27, Mark 13:34-37

THE SAME SPIRIT -- NO 1

1 Cor 3:1-4 2:7-10 Rom 1:4 Eph 1:19-21 Rom 6:5

I Cor 3:1-4 Walk as men (mere mortal men) plain, ordinary, common, everyday men! (Controlled and dominated by the flesh) *One of the saddest facts *Why? No understanding of Resurrection. (Symbol not manger or cross = Open, empty grave) Resurrection is the keystone of Christianity.

2:7-10 Unto our Glory. *(Jesus did it all for us)

:8 Because of Resurrection. "Man would have ignored Calvary without Resurrection" (hates more than anything)

:9 Born again you have a million times more then what you think!

:10 Deep profound -- heavy

Eph 3:8 Unsearchable-bottomless-riches-wealth of Christ.

Rom 1:3&4 Demonstrated -- So much power was released that it shook foundations of Hell and Earth.

Col 2:15 Spoiled principalities and powers (conquered all the forces of darkness and left paralyzed and broken)

Rev 1:18 Keys of Death & Hell -- Broke the power of Sin!

Matt 28:18 All power (authority) been given unto Jesus in Heaven and Earth (universal dominion). *Broke satan's dominion over us, Spirit-soul-body. Complete liberation.

Eph 1:19-21 Over and above = the Resurrection (Exceeding greatness of His power) (Phil 2:9-11 Every knee will bow) (Col 1:15-19 All fullness dwell)

:19 His power to us ward = Same life that flowed through Jesus, flows through us. (Absolute control over every satanic attack)

Rom 8:11 Same Spirit (overcome sin, death, hell & devil) Dwells in us.

Rom 8:17 Heirs and Joint heirs. We are in union (oneness) with deity.

Eph 2:6 Seated together with Jesus.

I Jhn 3:2 Beloved now are we the Sons of God not mere mortal men.

I Jhn 4:4 Ye are of God, and hove overcome them; because greater is He etc. The ability of God that is in us, is utterly limitless. Channels whereby God's fullness pours out.

I Jhn 4:17 As He is so are we in this world. Satan recognizes we are his rulers, because of Jesus.

Rom 6:5 All that God is, is at our disposal (But must die to fleshy) SPEAKING WORD (John 2 = Jesus)

Rom 8:19 All of creation is in travail -- waiting for the manifestation of the Son's of God. Do not walk, think, talk as mere mortal men. Same Spirit in US

THE SHEPHARD KING

I Cor 4:8 Reigned as kings. Conquers, kings, overcomers, champions, and giant killers.

Rev 1:6 & 5:10 Made us Kings and Priests

Ps 47:3 He shall subdue the people under us, and the nations under our feet.

Rom 8:17 Heirs, heirs of God and joint heirs.

Zec 10:5 They shall be as mighty men, which tread down their enemies in the mire of the streets in the battle and they shall fight because the Lord is with them.

I Sam 16:07 On the heart, **Prov 4:23** keep they heart with all diligence; for out of it are issues of Life.

:13 Anointed Him, that day forward: guiding, protecting, empowering. Three (3) anointing's. 1) Brethren 2) Judah 3) Israel

I Sam 17:28 Eliab put down his brother, age, task, heart, reason for coming. *Knew anointed to be King.

:29 Cause reason, purpose, mission, job, task at hand, [would not allow self to be discouraged] Excited, enthusiastic, eager, committed. Takes faith to get involved. (Don't away or ignore giants)

Jam 4:7 Resist the devil.

:34-36 Lion and Bear, prevailed, won, overcame, anointing of a king upon him. Knew who was with him and who he was in God. Volunteered upon himself willing to eager.

:51 Came to grips with enemy. Ps 138:3 In the day when I cried thou answeredst me, and strengthens me, with strength in my soul. You don't have to be a big shot to set people free.

II Sam 11:1 Kings go forth to battle. Responsibility, duty, calling, position demanded it.

Eph 6:12 For wrestle not etc. Sent: to direct to go and act, divorce, to separate, break away from. Tarried: procrastinate, dilly dally, loiter. *Shirk responsibilities, side step. Quitter, dropout, -- the same man who had a cause, was to deliver, lead. * Who could make king? No one! At one time total commitment. Forsake all and follow me. Ignore your duty. Leads to death. Idle - lukewarm, unprofitable, worthless, slothful, (hero-out of action) deceitfulness, playground of the devil.

:2 Evening tide: humdrum, nothing to do, dull, listlessness, lethargic, boredom opens door to sin. Inactivity breeds sin and defeat. What happens when we lose contact with God's purpose and plan. *The curse of those who achieve security.

Pro 10:4 He becometh poor that dealeth with a slack hand but the hand of the diligent maketh rich.

Ecc 10:18 By much slothfulness the building decayed and through idleness of the hands the house dropped thorough.

AROSE Restless, sleepless, looking for trouble.

WALK Prowl, roaming, hurt

SAW Watch, observe, look intently,

Jam 1:14 Every man is tempted.
Flesh never satisfied, had six wives.

:3 Inquired -- Sought after, seek

:4 Took -- snatch, seize, take way, say adultery.

:15 Killed Uriah, came out of shirking his responsibility.

Eph 6:12 For wrestle not etc.

TO DO, TO HAVE, TO BE -- NO 2

Joshua 1:5-8 Pro 4:20-22 Pro 6:22-23 Deut 11:18-22 I Tim 4:15,16

Joshua 1:8 To Do, To Have, To Be... How!
1) Thou 2) Strong, Courageous 3) Turn Not From

Turn Not First, must recognize the importance of -- before ever turn to it.

Matt 4:4 Man shall not live by bread alone.

Ps 19:7 The Law of the Lord is perfect converting the soul.

Ps 107:20 He sent His Word, and healed

Heb 1:3 He up holds all things by the Word of His power.

1 Pet 1:22 Born of the incorruptible word of life.

Must Desire

1 Pet 2:2 Desire the sincere milk of the Word.

Ps 119:103 How sweet are thy words unto my taste, yea, sweeter than honey to my mouth.

Jer 15:16 Thy words were found, and did eat the, and thy word was unto me the joy and rejoicing of mine heart.

Ps 1:1-3 Blessed is the man, etc... You cannot believe beyond the knowledge of God's Word that you have hid in your heart. Don't treat the Bible or the cross like a rabbits foot. If you are going to carry it, read and believe it. If you are going to wear it, proclaim and preach it. Only those who know, believe, act on it, will obtain Biblical prosperity and success. It must be the rule, law conduct, and thoughts of our lives.

Pr 4:20-22 Life, Health, to those who find. 6:22-23 Lead, keep talk with thee

Joshua 1:8 Clarifies Point III. In your mouth == Rom 10:18 But what saith it? The word is night thee even in thy mouth and in your heart; That is the word of faith, which we preach.

Eph 5:19 Speaking to yourselves in psalms and hymns and spiritual songs, singing and making melody in your heart to the Lord.

Ps 19:14 Let the words of my mouth and the meditation of my heart, be acceptable in thy sight, O Lord my, etc. Mediate: reflect, ponder, concentrate, revolve, think on (heavy) stew over, brood over. Example: Chicken over eggs! Check kind of eggs sitting on.

Job 3:25 Negative -- Worry, fear, bitterness, lust, etc... Chew the cud. Ex: Cow, grass, milk. Speak out loud, mutter, converse with self.

James 3:2 Tongue is a bridle, a helm.

2 Tim 2:15 Study to show yourselves approved unto God. ** Don't just glance at it, or give it a quick once over -- flip through the pages, skim over. Investigate, search, meat grinder, leave no stone unturned and no avenue unexplored. We are rejecting God when we refuse to read, study, speak the Word.

Deut **11:18:21** Rom 12:2 But be ye transformed. **Matt 12:34** out of the abundance of the heart.

Ps 119:11 Thy word have I hid in my heart, that I might not sin against thee. Storehouse "cannot overdose on God's Word" Whatever possess your mind -- ways your tongue. The best way to teach the Word is to live it.

:21 Heaven on earth.

1 Tim 4:15,16 Profiting may appear unto all.

TO DO, TO HAVE, TO BE! NO 1

Joshua 1:6-8 Deut 11:18-26 I Tim 4:15-16

Rom 7:19 To be a doer. You can be! For the good that I would I do not; but the evil which I would not, that I do. Oh Happy Days.

James 1:22 Be a Doer and not just a Hearer. DOER = performer, practitioner, worker, laborer, bread winner, roustabout, a believer -- you say I am and I say are you! How about?

Mr 16:17 These signs shall follow

Ways will be prosperous -- to be whole, sound, safe, well off, flourish, thrive, well-to-do, partaking of the milk and honey (God promised us) Make progress, headway, blossom, grow fat.

Ps 92:12 The righteous shall flourish like the palm tree, he shall grow like a cedar in Lebanon.

:13 Those that be planted in the house of the Lord shall flourish in the courts of our God.

:14 They shall still bring forth fruit in old age: they shall be fat and flourishing;

Pr 13:4 The soul of the diligent shall be made fat. It is biblical to be fat. I am testing.

Ps 122:6 They shall prosper that love thee.

3 John 2 I wish above all things that thou mayest prosper and be in health, even as thy soul prospereth.

Ps 35:27 The Lord hath pleasure in the prosperity of His servants. (God wants us to prosper in the realm of the

Spirit, Soul, Body.

2 Tim 4:7 Have good success: to take possession, to inherit, to accomplish, possess, victory, prevail, achieve one's purpose, to reach the goal. I have fought a good fight. I have finished my course, I have the faith.

John 19:30 Jesus finished His mission. To be on the top, to prevail over.

We can do, can have, can be! How? Listen up -- undivided attention, become all ears. State requirements.

Thou -- 9 times, telling us it is in our hands. Personal, self, ball is in your court, yours truly, you all. You determine to do, to have, to be. Not in our ability but His. Adam blamed Eve for his failure, who have you been or what have you been blaming? The destiny of your life is in the palms of your hands. You determine. (Job, Joseph, Daniel, Jesus -- lifted up out of it.)

Eph 6:10 Strong, very courageous have to be. Be strong in the Lord. Manly vigor, firm, to hold fast to, to be determined, unwavering, non-compromising (to make up your mind.)

2 Tim 1:7 Courageous: To be fearless God has not given us a spirit of fear to be bold brave. Confident in God, spiritual backbone, take the bull by the horns. Keep a stiff upper lip, daring, audacious. **Matt 11:12** And from the days of John the Baptist until now the kingdom of heaven suffereth violence, and the violent taketh by force. (Some guts). Not pansy's and sissy's.

Ps 119:103 How sweet are thy words unto my taste, yea; sweeter than honey to my mouth.

Jer 15:16 Thy words were found, and I did eat them and they word was unto me the joy and rejoicing of mine heart.

Ps 1:2 His delight is in the Law of the Lord. I do not believe that we have really grasped a hold of the importance of God's Word in our lives. We have got to desire to be in line with the Word. The Word of God is the living food upon which this life has got to feed. All of our decisions must be based upon God's Word. Let the world cause you to prosper and succeed.

Jhn 8:32 You shall know the truth, and the truth shall make you free.

I Pet 2:2 Desire the sincere milk of the Word.

Matt 4:4 Man shall not live by bread alone. The Word needs to be the final authority in our lives. I wonder how many are truly depending upon God's Word to cause them to prosper and succeed in life. If the amount of knowledge that you know to possess your present job was equivalent to the workable knowledge you have of God's Word--Would you prosper and succeed, or would you starve to death?

CHAPTER FIVE

WALKING ON THE WATER

MATT 14:22-33

MATT 14:24 Tossed=Torture vex contrary=against, opposite waves is daily circumstances, wind is the devil.

Matt 14:25 Walking = To trample down under foot for Jesus walking above, not below circumstances.

Matt 14:26 A lot of Christians afraid of tongues and gifts.

Matt 14:27 Cheer: Have courage boldness (daring) It is I that is setting the captives free.

Isaiah 41:10 Fear thou not; for I am with thee: be not dismayed; for I am thy God:

I will strengthen thee; yea, I will help thee; yea, I will uphold thee with the right hand of my righteous.

Matt 14:28 Bid: Order, command Peter says is Your will then tell me, is it God's will we are healed? etc.

Matt 14:29 Come. Bible tells us so! Once you know God's will. **ACT!**

James 1:22-24 Doer. Keep your eyes on the word of God. Look to Jesus the Author and Finisher of our Faith. Peter trampled under foot: the circumstances!

Matt 14:30 Saw: regard, take heed. Peter saw wind. Took eyes of Jesus and listened to devil. Then fear moves in, and Peter began to sink. When you start walking by Faith, keep your eyes on the Word and not the circumstances. Praise God, just in time Peter cried out and put his eyes back on Jesus or circumstances would have drowned him.

Matt 14:31 Get back on the Word, will receive help immediately. Little: Lacking confidence in Jesus. Wherefore: reached or entered. Peter didn't have to doubt. All you need is Faith the size of mustard seed.

James 1:5 If any of you lack wisdom let him ask of God, that giveth to all men liberally, and upbraideth not; and it shall be given him.

James 1:6-7 But let him ask in faith, nothing wavering. For he that wavereth is like a wave of the sea driven with the wind and tossed. For let not that man think that he shall receive any thing of the Lord.

Matt 14:32 Wind ceased. Slowly diminished. Resist the devil and he shall flee. Always going to be trials because we are in the world.

Matt 14:33 Overcome and it will glorify God.

ADVERSARY - OUT LINES

DEVIL

OVERCOMING THE DEVIL

II COR 2:10&11 10:3 ISA 14:12-17 JHN 8:44 11 COR 11:12-15

:11 Advantage -- outsmarted, get the victory, superiority, upperhand, the better.

HOS 4:6 Cut off of His thoughts, purposes, and designs, plans, ignorant. Blind, hard, wicked, stupid, unperceiving. *Knowledge "Godly, biblical" will set us free. **(Spiritual intelligence) (if we are ignorant to the devil and his devices and strategies not ready for battle) (source of all Christian opposition)**

:3-4 Take the devil seriously, spiritual warfare!

ISA 14:12-17 Lucifer: light bringer or shining one.
*Hates the Saints because they have his job.

Singing! and desire that is to be like the most high.

:14 Wanted to be the Most High. **(Always looking for a throne to sit on)** *Carbon copies God, spoke.

:16-17 **JHN 10:10** a murder, no sympathy, psychopathic killer!

JHN 8:43-44 Many sinners suppress their satanic nature, just like many Christian suppress their Godly natures.

:43 The revelation was beyond their comprehension.

:44 Adversary, was not rooted and founded in the Truth speaks what's false, doing that which is natural to him.

II COR 11 Masquerading, counterfeits.

:12-15 *Need to wake up to the deceits, tricks deceptions, lies of the devil.

OVERCOMING THE DEVIL -- NO. 2

II COR 12:7-10 Thorn in the flesh **(only one Satan can give)** Messenger of satan. To buffet: beat, slap, punch, strike. **(Will come against us)** *To stop the preaching of the Gospel, wants to get in our way.

PROV 11:9 ***Through knowledge shall the just be delivered....***

:9&10 In not for.

ROM 8:28 ***And we know all things work together for good to them that love God, to them who are the called according to his purpose.***

If you will exercise your authority, believe and trust God, He can turn any situation around. Always have the upper hand.

ROM 16:20 And the God of peace shall bruise **(crush)** Satan under your feet shortly.

Satan gets to us through people and circumstances. New creation is master of satan and demons.

PS 8:2***Mouth of babes ...***

(Satan wants to cause our downfall) Wants to inhibit, repress, suppress, weaken, delayed. **(The devil may put a tear in your eyes, but if you will trust and obey God. It will turn into a rainbow.)**

VICTORY OVER THE DEVIL -- NUMBER 3

EPH 6:10-12 DANIEL 10:11-13 II COR 12:7-10 ROM 8:28

:10 Finally: conclusion once for and for all.
Might: boundless resources.

:11 Wiles of the devil. Strategies, tricks, devices, schemes, deceptions.

:12 **(Not flesh and blood)** The source of all Christian opposition. Take the devil and his demonic host seriously,

:11 He is seeking, plotting and coniving to bring about our destruction.

EPH 4:27*Neither give place to the devil.*

*The devil will try every trick in the book and more to cause our down fall.

II COR 10:3*For though we walk in the flesh, we do not war after the flesh .....*

Satanic forces that are using flesh and blood against us.

The world and flesh and blood is the ammunition, weapons, arsenal. Four distinct levels of satanic power. Just because you can't see doesn't mean any less dangerous, but more so! Wrestle **(Do not just give in)** take by force what belongs to you in the spirit realm.

Hand to hand combat with an opponent. Do you pin him to the floor. **(Vibrate)** shake loose and pin. Out manuver. **(Many are wrestling with everything else but the devil)**

*Takes training to win a wrestling match, endurance! Know the right moves. Give in for just a minute you are pinned. Give into the lies of the devil same. Know your opponent.

READ Daniel 10:11-13

Greatly beloved, also verse 19

:12 First day **(hear it is three weeks later and no answer)**

:13 Withstood: oppose, defied, confronted, **(intercepted, delayed, hindered, retarded the answer to Daniels prayer.)** 1 & 21 days long

Satan will always try to throw a monkey wrench in the gear works! Wants to stunt our growth, retard our spritual progression and cause our downfall.

I THES 2:18*Wherefore we would have come unto you, even I Paul, once and again: but Satan hindered us.*

Daniel did not give in or quit! **(Do not throw in the towel)** *Many Christain do not really realize or recognize that it is Satan that hinders immediate physical manifestations.

Jesus always had immediate results because He was consistently and vigourously attacking the satanic realms.

MATT 11:12*The kingdom of heaven sufferth violence and the violent take it by force.*

VICTORY OVER THE DEVIL -- NUMBER 4

ZEC 3:1 II COR 12:7-10 JAMES 4:7-10 ROM 8:28 16:20

ZEC 3:1 Standing at his side to resist, oppose, hinder. *Throw a monkey wrench in the gear works! Inhibit, repress, weaken.

II COR 12:7-10 Thorn in the flesh, (only kind) Messenger of Satan! **(Buffet: beat, slap, punch, strike, harsh, hinder, (obstruct, block, inhibit, impede)**

PRO 11:9 Through knowledge shall the just be delivered.

:8 Recognized satanic attack

11:23-28 Influenced by devil

:9 You have a tremendous amount to do with

making and keeping yourself free.

(Do not let the devil give you the run around)

:10 God will exalt!

ROM 8:28 Love and know. Purpose: walking in His plans! The devil may put a tear in your eye, but if you will do the word it will turn into a rainbow.

VICTORY OVER THE DEVIL -- NUMBER 5

LU 4:1-14, I JHN 2:15-17, I COR 10:12&13

:1 Systematically. Absolute, imperative necessity.

EPH 3:19 Be filled with the fullness of God!

EPH 5:18 Be filled with the Spirit **(Yield yourself to be full of)** *Prepared, equipped, furnished, for combat, fortified against Satan's assaults. **(Preventive medicine)**

WILDERNESS -- only promotes people He can't trust!

JAMES 1:13 ***Let no man....***

:2 Where ever God is at work -- you can guarantee you will find the devil! **(seeking, plotting, conniving)** *The richest treasures are the thief's No. 1 Desires!

I JHN 2:15-17 Three predominant classes, main categories.

A. Appetite of the desires of the flesh.

B. Greedy longings of the mind

C. No. 1 self-reliance. Exalting self, talking about self, wanting honor and applause!

*Satan is a master at ringing peoples chimes.

(Lie down with the skunk, you will get up smelling like one.) :17

READ JAMES 1:22

LU 4:3 If thou **(know He was)** try to get us to doubt our sonship.

Healed! Blessed! etc. *Attacked Jesus where He was, His weakest point!

:4 Written: "did not speak His body" **(do not let your body talk)** You will be a prisoner of the devil.

HEB 4:12 Spoke the Word.

READ EPH 6:18

:7 Satan is as phoney as a three-dollar bill or a wooden nickel! Promises everything, gives nothing. To keep away from God. No **(short cut to the fulfilling of God's will "a lie")**

:8 Take authority over the devil! Worship is done with the lips!

(Cannot send devil to hell)

:13 Satan is limited. Departed not far off.

I COR 10:12-13 Ordinary, common, everyday trials, test, temptations! Flesh and blood.

PS 91:3*Surely he shall deliver thee from the snare of the follower....*

II PET 2:9*The Lord knoweth how to deliver the Godly out of temptations....*

LU 10:19 Behold, I give **(We do not need to perplex ourselves with the difficulties that lie in our pathway, when we have God on our side)**

VICTORY OVER THE DEVIL -- NUMBER 6

MARK 5:1-15 & 20

:2 Immediately. **(First devil will come against you. Second people with needs all around) Jhn 10:10**

Unclean: drive you to defile, contaminate, pollute, corrupt yourself! Takes elbow grease to get clean.

:3 Among dead: will try to keep us away from flock.
*No man **(spiritual problem)** psychologist, mental institutions, drugs. Never pills, doctors not the answer!

:4 Could not change, restrain, control, discipline themselves.

READ ROM 7:15-25 (Praise God through Jesus Christ)

JAMES 4:7 Submit to God.

:5 In torment. People need deliverance! Oppressed, obsessed, possessed. *Devil tries to get us to destroy ourselves! No. 1 weapon in devil's arsenal **(self destruct)** **(We are our own worst enemy)**

:6 Bowed and worshipped. "Demons sometimes worship God more than some believers do"

:7 If the devil and demons do how much more should we!

JAMES 2:19 Devils also believe and tremble!

:8 Come out of the man, **(all sickness is influenced by satanic power)** Took authority over situation.

JOB 2:7 Body, soul, spirit! **(*Birds over head, but not on your head)**

:9 Legion is strictly a military term! Warfare.
:13 Devil's drive you to death. "Their main goal"
(God leads us to life)

:15 Bondage, broken, right mind.

II TIM 1:7 Sound mind: when loose, influenced by devil. **(PHIL**

4:8)

A)Exercise authority you have in and through Jesus. **MATT 18:18&19**

B)Get filled with God's Word.

C)Preach, proclaim Gospel -- God's tool

TESTED, TEMPTED, AND TRIED

JAMES 1:1-4, :12 4:6-10

Pride -- Door way into a carnal heart! Proud, arrogant, self-centered, sufficient, made

PRO 16:18 ***Pride goeth before destruction.***

*Pride turned angels into devils! **(Root of all sin) (To exalt self, superior, above others, better)** haughty, arrogant

ISA 14:12-15 **(Five times I)** Good confession

JAM 4:3 ***Ye ask,***

MATT 23:12***Whosoever shall exalt himself shall be abased: and he that shall humble himself shall be exalted.***

*Last generation.

II TIM 3:2***For man shall be lovers of their ownselves, covetous, boasters, proud, blasphemers, disobedient to parents, unthankful , unholy.***

ISA 13:6

EZE 16:49 Iniquity of Sodom was pridefulness of bread, abundance of idleness, did not help the poor and needy.

PS 10:2***The wicked in his pride doth persecute the poor ...***

DEUT 8:1 Live, multiply, and possess

:2 To humble, to prove, know what in thine heart

:3 **MATT 5:3** ***Blessed is the poor in spirit: for theirs is the kingdom of heaven.***

MATT 11:29***Take my yoke upon you, and learn of me: for I am meek and lowly in heart and ye shall find rest unto your souls.***

PRO 22:4***By humility and the fear of the Lord are riches, honor, and life.***

II CHR 7:14***If my people, which are called by my name, shall humble...***

ISA 57:15***For thus saith the high and lofty One that inhabiteth eternity, whose name is Holy: I dwell in the high and holy place, with him also that is of a contrite and humble spirit, to revive the spirit of the humble, and to revive the heart of the contrite ones.***

I PET 5:4***And when the chief Shepherd shall appear, ye shall receive a crown of glory that fadeth not away.***

Clothed in humility **(to have a humble opinion of yourself)** a deep sense of ones moral littleness, lowliness of mind.

PHIL 2: ***Let every man esteem others better them ....***

To behave in assuming manner. Grace to the humble.

:6 Humble yourself

:9 Cannot resist the humble

TESTED, TEMPTED, AND TRIED #2

ZERO TOLERANCE

JAMES 1:2-3 Temptations

:12 Blessed: happy well off fortunate, to be envied. Endureth: steadfast **(cursed is he who falls)** remains, abides, preserves, continues.

PRO 1:9,10***For they shall be an ornament of grace unto thy head, and chains about thy neck. My son, if sinners entice thee, consent thou not.***

In otherwards, my son if thou has come to serve the Lord, prepare for temptation.

JAM 4:10 Specific instructions, pertinent for today's society.

II TIM 3:16***All scripture is given by inspiration of God, and is profitable for doctrine, for reproof, for correction, for instruction in righteousness.***

4:2***Preach the word; be instant in season, out of season; reprove,rebuke, exhort with all long suffering and doctrine.***

:7 The devil?

:1-5 Demonically influenced, lust of the eyes, of the flesh, pride and cares of life. *Satan wants to defile, contaminate, pollute, corrupt us.

EPH 6:12***For we wrestle not against flesh and blood....***

JHN 10:10***The thief cometh not***

(Self-centered, wrong motives, living for self) (Old Adam)

GAL 5:19***Now the works of the flesh are manifest, which are these; Adultery, fornication, uncleanness, lasciviousness, Idolatry, witchcraft, hatred, variance, emulations, wrath, strife, seditions, heresies, Envyings, murders, drunkenness, revelings, and such like: of the which I tell you before, as I have also told you in time past, that they which do such things shall not inherit the kingdom of God.***

READ COL 3:4-10

EPH 4:27***Neither give place to the devil...***

:5 Proud. "Pride **(self)** is the beginning of sin **(a proud, arrogant, self made, self-sufficient person, intense, sincere, will not pray, read bible, witness, etc.)** or praise God. To dignified.

PRO 16:18*Pride goeth before destruction, and an haughty spirit before a fall.*

Grace to humble.

:10 Humble.

PRO 22:4*By humility and the fear of the Lord are riches and honor and life.*

*Humility is only road to God **(son)**

*Servant of all.
*Took upon himself form of a servant, humbled himself. Real humility is the recognition of your littleness, in so much as you are compared to God's greatness. *Where is the humble servant, *Blessed to give **(nothing sets a person so much out of the devils reach as humility)** Jonathan Edwards *The taller you build the deeper you must dig!

:7 Submit: yield, surrender, comply, turn yourself over to! Conform to who?

ROM 6:14 **Sin:** For sin shall not have dominion over you for ye are not under the law but under grace. Flesh.

ROM 8:4*Who walk not after the flesh, but after the Spirit.*

INTELLECT

PRO 3:5*Trust in the Lord with all thine heart;*

DEVIL

EPH 4:27 ***Neither give place to the devil.***

PS 1:1 ***Blessed is the man that walketh.***

Circumstances.

II COR 5:7***For we walk by faith, not by sight.***

ROM 6:16***Ye are the servants of whom you obey***

Most are slaves to sin, flesh, intellect, world circumstances, materialism, devil!

GOD: Mind, body, spirit.

EPH 6:10***Be strong in the Lord.***

II SAM 22:2***The Lord is my rock, and my fortress, and my deliverer.***

*Let God arise and his enemies be scattered.

Flee from you God inside minded, directed, controlled.

(Do not tolerate, pet, pamper ungodly things in your life)

TESTED OF GOD AND TEMPTED BY THE DEVIL

TEMPTED, TESTED, TRIED, PROVED, EXAMINED

LU 4:1 Led by Spirit, wilderness, "Trying of your Faith"

JAM 1:3 Knowing this that wanted to get out of Faith. Out of Word.

:2 Tempted of devil. Out of God's nature.

:14 Power of Spirit

Do not bend our knees to the devil

His afflictions

(What kind of metal) *Character, fiber, commitment, love, vision, motives.

2:1***My son if thou come to serve the Lord, prepare thyself for temptation.***

I PET 1:3-7 Temptation is the fire that brings up the scum of the heart. Devil wants to see what your made out of **(pressure squeeze pinch)** *Brings impurities to surface. Fire tries iron and temptation tries a just man.

JAMES 1:13 Tempted with evil

:15 Submit to the testing's of God, resist the temptations of the devil. Example: Rich young ruler, **(still all you got)** Disciples: **(come and follow me)**

Eat my flesh, drink my cup. Have to pass the test before you can go on! *God test us with obedience, devil with sin.

JAMES 4:7 Submit yourself therefore to God. Resist the devil *Every temptation is an opportunity to flee to God.

The best way to escape evil is to pursue good.

(When a man tries to resist temptation in his own abilities, he will not hold out long)

GEN 22:1-2 **:10-12** Now I know

HEB 11:17 By Faith Abraham, when he was tried **(being put to the test)**

DEUT 8:1-2 To prove thee **(it is easy to be committed when everything goes your way)**

:3 Suffered thee to hunger.

PS 78:18 And they tempted God in their heart by asking for food for their desire.

:16 Prove thee, To do thee good.

PHIL 4:11-13 Not that I speak in respect of want: for I have learned.

I PET 5:8-9 Your adversary.

HEB 2:17,18 Suffered and tempted.

In all points tempted **(do not tolerate, pet, pamper, ungoldy things in your life)**

JHN 14:30***The prince of this world cometh and hath nothing in me.***

MATT 6:13Lead us not into temptation but deliver us from evil.

MATT 26:41Watch and pray that ye enter not into temptation.

ROM 6:16Know ye not, that to whom ye yield*...*

EPH 4:27*Neither give place to the devil.*

HEB 5:6-8*Learned obedience.* ***(Applied the Word)***

Phil 2:8 Became obedient unto death. "Not my will but your will be done"

PRO 11:9 Through knowledge shall the just be delivered.

*Not what comes to you that makes or breaks you, but how react, respond, what you do.

HEB 12:1-4 Resisted into blood.

ROM 8:18***For I reckon the sufferings of this present time are not to be***

compared with the glory which shall be revelaed in us.

Indulgence is way of flesh, discipline and order is way of the Spirit.

PS 119:133***Let not any iniquity have dominion over me.***

CHAPTER SIX

Temperance

Temperance is the proof that Jesus is MY Lord! Many of the problems that Christians get into, are caused by not saying no to their flesh! Discipline is a major aspect of the Christian life. Many broken friendships, and many harsh words come, as a result of not learning how to be temperate. Too many Christians take the attitude that they cannot control their temper, their thoughts, or their actions. This is simply not true. With God's Holy Spirit, and the promises of God we can practice temperance. The meaning of Temperance is being able to master your own desires and passions – to not be controlled by fleshly desires and passions! In the military as soldier we must live in strict discipline – so that we can WIN the war!

***Titus 1:7 For a bishop must be blameless, as the steward of God; not selfwilled, not soon angry, not given to wine, no striker, not given to filthy lucre;8 But a lover of hospitality, a lover of good men, sober, just, holy, temperate;9 Holding fast the faithful word as he hath been taught, that he may be able by sound doctrine both to exhort and to convince the gainsayers.**

TEMPERANCE is bringing all of your flesh under the absolute control of Jesus Christ, being Sober, and vigilant. The ability to say:

"No To The World, No to the Flesh, and No to the devil"

Temperance is a Gift from God (2Tim 1:7) Temperance is Something that must be Worked at (2Pet 1:5,6) A good example of Temperance (Dan 1:8-16)

***Acts 24:25 And as he reasoned of righteousness, temperance, and judgment to come, Felix trembled, and answered, Go thy way for this time; when I have a convenient season, I will call for thee.**

***1 Corinthians 9:25 And every man that striveth for the mastery is temperate in all things. Now they do it to obtain a corruptible crown; but we an incorruptible.**

***1 Corinthians 12:24 For our comely parts have no need: but God hath tempered the body together, having given more abundant honour to that part which lacked.**

***Galatians 5:23 Meekness, temperance: against such there is no law.**

***Titus 1:8 But a lover of hospitality, a lover of good men, sober, just, holy, temperate;**

***Titus 2:2 That the aged men be sober, grave, temperate, sound in faith, in charity, in patience.**

***2 Peter 1:6 And to knowledge temperance; and to temperance patience; and to patience godliness;**

***1 Corinthians 9:27 - But I keep under my body, and bring [it] into subjection: lest that by any means, when I have preached to others, I myself should be a castaway.**

***Galatians 5:22-25 - But the fruit of the Spirit is love, joy, peace, longsuffering, gentleness, goodness, faith, (Read More...)**

***Titus 2:12 - Teaching us that, denying ungodliness and worldly lusts, we should live soberly, righteously, and godly, in this present world;**

***2 Peter 1:6 - And to knowledge temperance; and to temperance patience; and to patience godliness;**

***Romans 12:1-2 - I beseech you therefore, brethren, by the mercies of God, that ye present your bodies a living sacrifice, holy, acceptable unto God, [which is] your reasonable service. (Read More...)**

***Romans 13:14 - But put ye on the Lord Jesus Christ, and make not provision for the flesh, to [fulfil] the lusts [thereof].**

***Proverbs 25:16 - Hast thou found honey? eat so much as is sufficient for thee, lest thou be filled therewith, and vomit it.**

***1 Peter 5:8 - Be sober, be vigilant; because your adversary the devil, as a roaring lion, walketh about, seeking whom he may devour:**

***1 Corinthians 9:25 - And every man that striveth for the mastery is temperate in all things. Now they [do it] to obtain a corruptible crown; but we an incorruptible.**

LIVING LIKE AN ANIMAL

DANIEL 4:27-37

Nebuchadnezzar had a dream from God. Warning. God always tells what the end results will be of doing and not doing. **:30** [1] Looking at himself and the physical things (got his eyes off of God and put them on world) -- always go hand in hand. Either fear, pride, lust or hatred (eyes) (flesh) **(pride)** **I JHN 2:16** **COL 3:1** ***If ye then be risen with Christ, seek those things which are above, where ....***

Wrong attitude, strutting, and vaunting (forgot about God!) *Self-sufficient, independent (show by your actions what you believe) Do not have time for God and Word because really believe can make it on our own. **I COR 10:12** ***Wherefore let him that thinketh he stand take heed lest he fall.*** **(PRO 28:28, LU 1:52, PR 16:18)**

:33 When you are deceived into thinking everything is going to be just fine -- without God and Word being first place. Your headed for trouble.

Lost mind, insane, mentally deranged, loose your spiritual identity, loose your spiritual faculties, and become unbalanced. *Forget who he was, lost his identity, became someone he wasn't became void of understanding.

[2] Driven from his possessions, heritage. [3] Started to live way below the standard of a king. [4] Think like an animal. Began to a) live, b) think, c) speak, d) eat, and e) act like an animal!

:32 Stayed in this condition until he recognized God as Lord of his life. **I COR 6:20** ***For ye are bought with a price; therefore glorify God in your body, and in your spirit, which are God's.***

:34 JHN 11:41, PS 123:1, He lifted eyes to heaven, understanding returned. **a)** Bless, praise and honor the Lord. **"OBEY" :36** Same time, established in his possessions when he put God first. ***MATT 6:33 Seek ye first the kingdom of God*** **....** Saw who he was, knew who he was, who he was because of God. Can expect God's blessings when we dutifully acknowledge God's title to and dominion over us and all we have.

CHAINS OF TORMENT

MRK 5:1-8 then 20

:2 Demon possessed (Man kind being bombarded) "Take devil seriously" Be aware of adversary.

EPH 6 & 2 COR 10:4 Satan is author of fear, worry, depression, sickness, discourage, self pity.

:3&4 Any man! Spiritual warfare! "Problem in spiritual realm psychologist, mental institutions are not the answers. Doters, surface, substitution, compromise, jimmy rig.

:5 Torment, had that man locked in chains, people tormented night and day all over world! (Need deliverance) "Satan gets to you through people and circumstances"

3 Steps: **Oppression** (depressed, sick, despair, fear, etc.) **Obsession** (in mental realm) **Possession** (controls spirit, soul and body) **:7** Satan fears Jesus, but still stay. Ex: (Reap what you sow) **:8** On the way out **(Jesus)** **:13** Satan and demons drive people to death (teenagers) Drugs, sex, worry. God leads us to life. **:15** Bondage broken, right mind! Torment is gone (Jesus) **2 TIM 1:7** Power, love, sound mind!

1) Exercise the rights and privileges. **:20** Use the name of Jesus, get filled with the Word, and publish the Gospel. **MATT 18:18&19** To bind and loose.

2) Meditate. Get filled Word. **JOS 1:8** Spirit and mind. **3)** Preach, publish and proclaim Gospel **PS 109:20** Tool of God.

CELESTIAL TROUBLE SHOOTERS -- NUMBER 2

ACTS 14:23, MAT 13:20-21, HEB 11:32-39, HAB 3:17-18, 2 TIM 4:18

MATT 13:20-21 Not root in himself. Rootage, word doesn't take root. Because: By reason of, owing to. But is by nature a temporizer, the pressure of circumstances.
I THES 1:5&6 Having welcomed the Word while under much pressure of affliction.
ROM 5:3 Tribulation worketh patience. **LUK 21:19** In your patience, possess ye your souls. (Christians should be like tea... Real strength is brought out in hot water)
HEB 11:32-39 Was a result of living, believing in, and acting on **GOD'S WORD**.
2 COR 4:16 ***For which cause we faint not; but though our outward man perish, yet the inward man is renewed day by day.*** (The devil may put a tear in our eyes but if you will yield to God, he will put a rainbow in your heart.)

HAB 3:17-19 All of his life is wrapped up in God. ***PS 55:22 Cast thy burden upon the Lord.*** **2 TIM 4:18** ***And the Lord shall deliver me from every evil work, and will preserve me unto his heavenly kingdom; to whom be glory for ever and ever.*** Trouble is like an little ugly dog. Looks bad coming at you. But looks silly when its running from you.

THE DEVOUR

EZEK 28:13-17 Have to know your enemy and his tactics **I PETER 5:8** Your adversary the devil **JHN 10:10** ***The thief cometh not, but for to steal***
LU 8:30--33 2,000 swine choked! Mass suicide. Devils ultimate goal is to drive you to death. (wants to possess you to kill you) We cannot send them to hell.

LU 22:31,32 Behold: look realize, wake up. The devil wants you to sift.
1 Frustration 2 Imitation [3] Deception [4] Affliction [5] Possession (Did Job -- could have stopped Satan, but didn't)

DEWORMED

ISA 5:3-7

:4 What more could do? Given unto us all things that pertains to life and to Godliness. **2 PET 1:4** ***Whereby are given unto us exceeding great and precious promises: that by these ye might be partakers of the divine nature, having escaped the corruption that is in the world through lust.*** *No excuse" Owner frustrated!
"Shed His blood, sent the Holy Ghost, gave His Word and nature, etc.

MATT 7:18,17,16

[II] **MATT 7:18,17,16** Fruit grows, not given. (Amplified) **JAMES 3:11**
Fountain sweet and bitter? **:12** Fig: Olive berries? Vine--figs? *Not from recreated Spirit! From flesh. **MR 4:3-20** **MR 4:3-9** **:7** yielded no fruit. **:18&19** Cares, riches, lusts *Lie down with pigs get up with worms. World the flesh and devil will lead you away from GOD! SIN is like a soft bed, easy to get into, but hard to get of! **GAL 5:16-25**. **I PET 2:11**. ***Dearly beloved, I beseech you as strangers and pilgrims abstain from fleshly lusts, which war against the soul.***

SEVEN (7) MAJOR ENEMIES: [1] Soil hard -- heart [2] Wet soil -- flaky spirituality [3] Frost [4] Hail [5] Mice strip bark = little foxes, bad attitudes. [6] (dear?) eat young, answer soap bars or hair balls, word and God's presence. [7] Bugs-demonic temptations. Every week for (6) weeks and once every 10 days use to be only 3 times a season -- 5 times worse (forsake not the)

A CLOSED DOOR

EPH 4:26-27. **(I Pet 5:8 Who he may devour)** Give place: Opportunity, foothold, handgrip, loophole. You and I have a tremendous amount to do with keeping the door shut on the devil. (Ignorance, unbelief, rebellion) ***For the thing which I greatly feared is come upon me, and that which I was afraid of is come unto me.***

JHN 14:30 We are responsible to deal with what gave place to the devil. **JHN 14:30** No claim, nothing in common, belonging to him, no power over me!

I SAM 13:14 Sought a man after his own heart. **(Tempted, but without sin)**

LU 22:3 Satan enter into Judas. How? Gave, place, wrong, ambitions. *Tried to cover up ungodliness **(should have fed poor)**

ACTS 5:3 Why hath Satan filled your heart? Responsible for decisions, attitudes, actions, priorities. Don't pet, pamper, tolerate, excuse ungodly, attitudes, priorities!

ROM 6:16 Ye are the servant to whom you obey. Like a bed, easy to get into, but hard to get out. **Mr. 7:18-23**. Like a wagon, no brakes, going down hill, longer you ride more dangerous it gets.

MR 7:18-23. (Heart is the will of your soul) Behind very ungodly attitude, motive, word, action, a satanic influence.

PS 81:12 ***So I gave them up unto their own hearts lust and they walked in their counsels.***

DRY PLACES

LU 11:14,26

:14 Devil goes. So will affliction. Spend all money on doctors, never healed. (Speak to Spirit then to body) Ex: Philippians **:15-16** Tempting (instigated inspired of Satan) Three most common rules. [a] Tempter (Anointing, position, authority)
[b] Deceiver [c] Accuser [d] Stealer [e] Destroyer Before God, God before us, before each other. To ourselves, Satan seeks to keep us in conscious to rob us of our

God consciousness. **:23** Not with, is against, **(siding and believing)** **:24** Unclean **(22)** foul, familiar, lying, seducing, jealous. Dry place, waterless, spirit, dry. Rest: ample of a place. Spiritual deserts are the breeding grounds of demons, attitudes, emotions, feelings, priorities. **2 PET 2:17** Walks without water. **JUDE 12** Clouds without water. (Not submitted to God) ***EPH 5:18 And be not drunk with wine, wherein is excess; but be filled with the Spirit.*** **:26** Parasites, blood suckers, leaches, they thrive on peoples *Satan is always looking for more control over our lives! (Birds over head) Ungodly attitude, emotions, thoughts, etc

LU 23:33&34 Know not etc. (Do not know who he is or who is influencing them)
I JHN 4:1 Try the spirits, whether of God (smell it out) Ex: fish, chicken, popcorn, coffee. The words, actions, attitudes reveal the spirit your yielding to! ***EPH 6:12...wrestle not against flesh and blood.*** *Behind every ungodly attitude, motive, action, is a satanic influence. Do not become a tool, a chess piece, of the devils.
(Do not tolerate, pet, pamper, ungodly things in your lives) "Smells like hate, bitterness, pride, jealousy"

DO NOT FAINT

JONAH 3:10, 4:5-8 II COR 4:16-18, HEB 12:2-4, MATT 26:41

:5 Sat down content.

Gratify, satisfy, indulge, craving.

Started pleasing flesh, tickle, red danger light.

:6 Joy based on a thing. Hook, line and sinker.

:8 Wished He would die? FAINTED: Weary, tired, exhausted, out of breath!

Why! Wrapped up and entangled in affairs of Life!

(Fair weather Christians) "Never heard from Him again" Taken out of picture. Lazy: Stand still, dormant, inactive, slothful, inactive, frozen chosen, neglect, passivity, stagnent, sluggard.

II COR 4:16:18 **(11:23-28)** Perish: Progressively decaying. Looking at **"WORD"**.

HEB 12:2-4 *Looking unto Jesus. Consider, contemplate, joy, and strength.

"Lest ye be wearied and faint **(give up)** *Mental realm! Example: Candle suffocating in its own wax. **(More dead than alive)** worn out.

LUK 18:1-8 Pray. A privilege and duty. "If neglected, you are going to faint."

A. Ungodly, heathenistic, ignoramus of a judge?

B. Widow who wants justice.

:5 Widow like a battering ram! Example: Moses and Pharaoh. **(Wear the devil thin)**

Made up her mind.

A) Determined
B) Persistent
C) Patient **(Brought results)**

*Reason for failure: People give up to soon. **(A quitter never wins)**

:8 Faith that won't quit.

MATT 26:41 Watch. When we drive our cars, we must stay awake or become dead. **(Hard to wake up when in spiritual slumber)**

PRAYING Is important. Will not fall for temptation and will not faint.

DO NOT FAINT

LUKE 18:1-8, GAL 6:7-9 HEB 10:36 ISA 40:28-31 PS 27:13-14

Watch, pray, and be vigilant.

a. **Determined**
b. **Persistent**
c. **Patience**

Example: Moses

GAL 6:7-9 Always sowing either to flesh or to Spirit.

Plant cultivate and care for garden or weeds will take over *if faint **(give up)**

"Loose even that which you have labored to build"

Let us not slacken our exertions by reason of the weariness that comes with prolonged effort in habitually doing that which is right.

HEB 10:36 Patience: endurance, constancy, perseverance.
Will Of God!

ISA 40:28-31 Wait. **(To bind together, expectancy. Wrapped up in God)** *God is a rewarder. *Draw nigh

a) Wings: ability to go above.

b) Run: get up and go "spiritual adrenalin"

c) Walk: to be at peace in body, soul, and spirit.

TO REST IS TO REST IN GOD

PS 27:13&14 *Wait on the Lord*

c:\advrsary\faint2

FALLEN FROM WORKS

REV 2:1-5 Write to the churches, congratulating. **:7**Churches = work
EPH 2:8&9. By faith

:2 Works -- activity 10 times 294 times. "Labor, deed, ministry, perform, wrought, help" Labor: toil and activities.

(Grace of works) Fruit, natural out growth Patience: endurance Fiscal out growths of its natural characteristics

MATT 5:16 ***Let your light so shine before men, that they may see your good works and glorify your Father which is in heaven.***

REV 22:12 And behold, I come quickly and my reward is with me, to give every man according as his work shall be. (God of action, not a promoter of hibernation. Rewarder of diligent seekers)

Ex: Chicken and eagle. The transference of energy that is produced by the motion of the point of application of a force and is measured by multiplying the force and the displacement of its point of application in the line of action. Something produced on accomplished by effort, exertion, or exercise of skill. (Faith which will produce works of Love) **:4** Left lst love and left her works. **LUK 7:47** ***He that loveth little doeth little.*** **ECC 10:18** ***By much slothfulness the building decayeth and through idleness of the hands the house droppeth through.*** Our lives, families, churches, world. What will be according to what we do.

HEB 10:38,39 Do not give up ground, retreat, but advance, possess, conquer.

GAL 5:7 Ye did run well, who did hinder you that ye should not obey the truth? Some area given up. Good Samaritan program. Home groups. Prayer, involvement!

ACTS 15:38 Instead of accompanying them on active service Winners are people who form the habit of doing things losers hate to do.

AMOS 6:1 Woe to them that are at ease in Zion. Anybody can always think of reasons why they cannot. Its a cheap and easy religion that doesn't do anything.

AT HIS FEET

LUK 10:38-42 Received **(believed).** As a guest, not as a master.

:38 Her house. My life, money, business, **(I will do as I please.)**

:39 Sat. Planted, **(conscious decision)** Why? Heard: Listening. *Jesus was speaking, determined to hear what he had to say, "valuable to her" **(Where Martha?)** Body of Christ. *A time to sit.

:40 But **(worried about all she had to do)** *House work kept calling her, world, flesh, devil, calling us away from God demanding our attention.

PR 19:27*Cease, my son, to hear the instruction that causeth to err from the words of knowledge.*

She was totally engrossed, wrapped up, immersed, occupied in the physical.

:41 Careful and troubled. Priorities all mixed up, divided, your taking **(trying)** to walk in two different directions.

MR 3:24 Kingdom divided against itself.

REV 3:16 Neither cold, nor hot.

:42 Needful: Necessity, must, absolute, essential.

CHOSEN You choose, no one else can for you.

PS 119:30*I have chosen the way of truth; thy judgements have I laid before thee.*

PHIL 4:6*Be careful for nothing: but in every.* Not taken away.

MR 4:7 **:18** Hear, not receive.
:20 Receive: fruitful

:19 Entering in -- pushes out.

CARES Anxieties, worries, concerns, up to our ears with daily situations of life.

DECEITFULNESS Chokes, strangles, suffocates, and nullifies.

WORD Unfruitful, unproductive, none beneficial, barren, Spirit, wasteland, smothers the Word.

LUK 21:33 Not pass away.

:34 Anytime, overpowered, loaded down, lest your minds should ever be dulled, dissipation, self-indulgence, revelry. Catch you like the springing of a trip.

:35 Day will dawn on each and every man.

THE FINAL CONFRONTATION -- NUMBER 1

I **REV 12:7-12** War in heaven, Michael and his Angels fought, cast to earth. Battle isn't over 1/3rd rebelled, **(LU 24:29 flesh and bone)** War on earth.

2 COR 10:3 ***For though, we walk in the flesh, we do not war after the flesh....*** **EPH 6:12** ***For we wrestle not against flesh and blood but against....*** **I PET 5:8** ***Be sober, be vigilant: because your adversary the devil, as a roaring lion.*** **JHN 10:10** ***Thief cometh not but for to steal, and to kill, and to destroy***

2 COR 2:11 ***Lest Satan should get an advantage of us: for we are not ignorant of his devices.*** There is a conflict, battle, fight, war going on. (House of cards) Personal problems caused by demonic influence! Spirit-Soul-Body. The devil studies our weaknesses and uses them against us! (Look around you!) What are we to do? Are we lambs to the slaughter?

III Look at Paul. **2 TIM 4:2-8** **I TIM 6:12** ***Fight the good fight of faith ....*** **I COR 9:26** ***So fight I not as one the beateth the air....*** We must fight. **ROM 13:12** ***The night is far spent, the day is at hand, lets therefore cast off the works of darkness and let us put on the armor of light.*** **EPH 6:11** ***Put on the whole armor of God, that ye may be able to stand against the wiles of the devil.***

If you lose, it is because you did not fight or your relationship with God was lacking. People die, wounded, defeated because they do not fight the real enemy. **I COR 10:13** God always makes a way of escape. We have to confront evil, not compromise with it. (Final confrontation) Stop being ugly to each other, get ugly with the devil. *Change will not come without confrontation. Drive the enemy out of your territory. **2 COR 10:4** ***For the weapons of our warfare...*** We have weapons but do not use them.

IV **GEN 39:7-10** Joseph said no. **JUDGES 16:16,17** Samson played the devils game and lost. You will face your Deliah! Must bring every area of our life into absolute obedience to God and His Word. Quit finding excuses for our flesh. "Mind, emotions, feelings, flesh, confront evil do not comprise with it. The lines are being drawn. "Stick of dynamite"

V **JER 51:20&21** On the offensive, not defensive, Jesus was a man of action. Have to be cunning and wise in the Spirit. Do not wait for him to hit you first. Sock it to him, be determined to win, to do something for God. Be militant, invade the enemy's camp. Have to be cunning and wise in the Spirit. It is an invading force.
I PET 1:13 Gird your mind for action. **REV 12:11** ***And they overcome him by the blood of the Lamb.*** We need to become ruthless when it comes to the devil and His afflictions. ***2 SAM 22:40 For thou has girded me with strength to battle; them that rose up against me, hast thou subdued under me.***

VI **JER 12:5** The lines are being drawn. Faint hearted will not stand a chance. Blessed is a man who perseveres under trial. **2 TIM 3:1-7** Perilous times shall come.

THE FINAL CONFRONTATION NUMBER 2

REV 12:7 War. Not make believe, imaginary, fable, **(reality)** fierce battle, fight, struggles, conflict.

:8 Prevailed: Devil did not win, defeated, overcame, won.

:9 Deceiveth: beguiled, seduced, hood winked, duped, ensnared, tricked. Whole world **(do not under estimate devil)**

:10 Now: not when in heaven. *On earth as it is in heaven.

*Hour of Victory.

:11 Overcame: blood, spoken word, and lived not life.

:12 Rejoice. Woe to earth. Knoweth, short time **(war transferred to earth)** Knock down, dragged out, nasty fight. *Living in a time of over whelming problems, mental, emotional, social, economical, political, environmental, financial, physical, moral **(tip of iceberg)**.

EPH 6:12*For we wrestle not against flesh & blood (amp) but against.*

II COR 10:3*For though we walk in the flesh, we do not war after the flesh.*

I PET 5:8*Be sober, be vigilant (wake up, be on the alert) because your...*

JHN 10:10*The thief cometh not, but for to steal.*

Whether we like it or not, accept, believe, or not.

EPH 2:1,2 Prince: under the control, obeyed the devil. Disobedience will not believe or obey the truth, the will of God.

:3 Flesh, desires, indulged in the cravings of earthly nature, imaginations, impulses, dictates. *Demonized generation!
More than Noah's generation. *Hate, bitterness, resentment, unforgiveness, anti-Semitism, prejudice **(mental, emotional, sexual perversion, immorality)** lust for pleasure, materialism, greed, never satisfied. Fear, anxiety, depression. Sickness, disease, plagues, incurable ailments.

II TIM 3:1*This know also, that in the last days* ....

:7 Source, origin, root cause, birthing place, breeding

pond of all these are demonic powers. *They are blood suckers, leaches, parasites **(who thrive, live, exist on peoples ungodly thoughts actions, attitudes, emotions)**

*Can Christians be demonized, unequivocally, without a shadow of a doubt, absolutely yes **(not spirit, but soul, and body)** "We open the door by what we say, do read, watch, think, believe" Words call for spiritual powers!

EPH 4:27*Neither give place to the devil* (opportunity, foothold, handgrip)

ROM 13:12*The night is far spent, the day is at hand: let us therefore castoff the works of darkness and let us put on the armor of light.*

We must close the door, no permanent relief can be obtained unless we close the door. *We must get free, to set others free.

ACTS 10:38 Healing curing. All oppressed of devil: harassed, overpowered, under the influences. Demonized people, *Jesus: WORD ***When the anointing of God, the Word, Holy Ghost, and the power of God are in operation, satan's stronghold is broken!**

I JHN 3:8*For this purpose the Son of God was manifested*

II COR 3:17*The Spirit of the Lord is...*

ZEC 4:6*Not by might, nor by power.*

LU 4:18*The Spirit of the Lord is...*

II COR 10:4*For the weapons of our warfare...*

LU 10:18*And he said unto them, I beheld Satan as lightning fall from heaven.*:19*Behold, I give unto your power to tread ...*

LET GOD ARISE

A FOOL FOR CHRIST

I COR 4:6 Not to think **(arrogant champions)**

PR 26:12 Seest thou a man wise in his own conceit?

There is far more hope of a fool than of him.

I COR 3:18*Let no man deceive himself, if any man among you seemeth to be wise in this world, let him become a fool, that he may be wise.*

:7 Differ: preeminence, superior.

:8 Satisfied, rich.

:9 Criminals, men condemned to death

:10 Are you fools

1:18 Foolishness: folly to those on path to ruin.

:20 Utter folly

GAL 6:3*For if a man think himself to be something, when he is nothing, he decieveth himself.*

:25 Wiser than the wisest plan of the wisest man.

:26-27 Foolish: simpletons to put to shame

:28 Humble birth

:29 No place for human pride in the presence of God.

:30 Owe it all to Christ

:31 If going to boast, boast in the Lord **(Humility is death to self)**

ACTS 17:18 Rag picture, chatter box, charlatan

:32 Laugh ironically Paul could care less what they thought.

Rag picture, chatter box, charlatan

:32 Laugh ironically Paul could care less what they thought.

JAM 3:10 Not right, **:13** meekness = humility wisdom

:14-16 Earthly, devilish (**:17-18**)

GAL 5:22 But the Fruit of the Spirit Is Love...

TWELVE GATES OF NEW JERUSALEM

[I] **REV 21:2** As a bride (does not say bride) **EPH 5:25** Husbands love your wives,**:26, :27** ***That he might present...*** **:10** In spirit. **:12** Twelve gates, twelve angels, twelve tribes. **:13 & :14** Twelve foundations 12 = perfection of government of authority and rule. **:21** twelve pearls, {we are pearl of great price} *Typology of Church.

PS 24:7

[II] **PS 24:7** Ye gates, everlasting doors, **:8** & **:9** King of Glory come in -- we are the door Holy Ghost comes through to enter into world. **:10** King of Glory. *We must possess the gates. ***JHN 14:30 After this I will not talk much with you: for the prince of this world cometh, and hath nothing in me.***

LU 11:34

[III] **LU 11:34** Eye (if dark, full of darkness) Gate into your life, set nothing evil before eyes! Touch, taste, see, smell, hearing. Set no wicked before your eyes. If Satan can possess these gates -- has your life. Ex: Trojan horse = entertainment! ⑤ gates What flows in, flows out! {Close gates in darkness}

2 COR 4:4

[IV] **2 COR 4:4** The mind [6], emotions or feelings [7], will [8], imagination [attitude] [9]. *Music, drugs, alcohol opens these gates. **2 COR 11:14** Satan himself is transformed into an angel of light. **2 COR 11:3** Serpent bequiled Eve, so your minds. ***PS 1:1 Blessed is the man who walketh....***

PS 141:3

[V] **PS 141:3** Door of my lips (mouth opens doors, death and life [10])

PRO 6:24

[VI] **PRO 6:24-27** [11] Sex outside of marriage opens door to the devil, big time. Conscience [12] **I TIM 4:2** seared withhot iron. Purge conscience from dead works, hear sprinkled from an evil conscience.

HEAVENS PROVING GROUND

MATT 3:16-17 Moment he lived for!

4:1 Led by Spirit **(None involvement, self-fulfillment, spirit retirement)** No wilderness. Tempted of devil. "Testing time, examination, what are you made out of? What is in you? *Character, morals, vision, motives, fruit. Love and faith.

JAM 1:3 Knowing this that the trying of your faith...

ECCL 2:1? ***My son if thou come to serve the Lord prepare thyself for temptation.***

:2-4 Forty days, if thou be. It is written. "Had to get Jesus out of God's will, word, Faith in order to defeat" *Do not bend our knees, mind, emotions, desires to the devils nature or His afflictions!

I PET 1:3-7 :5 Kept: guarded, protected, maintained power of God. Faith must be exercised.

EPH 6:16 Above all...

:6 Manifold: under, the midst of many kinds of trials **(major exams)**

:7 Trial: proving and testing.

(Temptation is the fire that brings up the scum of the

heart) Pressure brings the impurities to the surface.

I PET 4:12,13 Strange: surprised and astonished.

Fiery trial, to test you! Taking place, being applied. Christ sufferings.

PHIL 3:10*That I might know him...*

ROM 8:18*For I reckon that the sufferings of this present.*

JAM 1:13 **(Everyone being tested)**

JAM 1:13 Tempted with evil **(to do wrong, immoral)** Neither in like fashion.

:14 Own lusts **(beguiled and lured by own desires)**

:15 Death!!!

JAM 4:7 Submit: subject, yield, surrender, comply, obey, conform, **(Spirit, soul, mind, body, emotions)** To who? Sin, flesh, world, lust, devil? No to god!

EPH 91:4*His truth shall be thy shield and buckler.*

EPH 6:10*Finally my brethren be strong*

2 PET 2:9 The Lord knoweth how to deliver the Godly out of temptation. "Let God arise and his enemies be scattered" Resist: military term, set oneself against, declare war, oppose, wage battle.

Stand firm, with stand, (immediate, consistent, boldly, vigorously, unceasingly) not spasmodic, no delay. *Passivity will kill you (cannot resist if not yielded)

When a man tries to resist evil, temptation on his own ability, won't hold out very long? Every temptation is an opportunity to flee to God! Best way to escape evil is to flee to pursue the Good!

GEN 22:1,2 God did tempt Abraham **(tested, tempted, tried, put under pressure)** Will God do that? Yes, big time!

HEB 11:17***By faith, Abraham, when he was tried.***

:2 Offer him. Example: Rich young ruler, disciples, **(Follow me)** Eat my flesh...

*Have to past the test before we can move on! God test us with obedience, commitment, faith. Devil with sin! Example: Kingdom of Heaven is like a man... 1 pound 2&3 To see

:10-12 Now I know (must love God more then your own family) It is easy to obey God, be committed when no pressure to the doing of it.

CHAPTER SEVEN

A DECEIVED HEART -- NO 2

MIND GAMES

You will believe a lie if listen to it long enough. Thoughts control your actions.

GEN 3:1-7 Pandora's Box. Subtle, crafty, clever, slick, devil, master, at manipulation and deception. Evil conniving games, smooth operator. Question: find out her knowledge and attitude. Example: Salesman and politicians. *Look for a way to enter or deposit his seeds into her mind.

LEST: per adventure, possibility "made the declaration of God a possibility instead of an inescapable result" **:4&5** Lied to her **(JHN 8:44 Father of lies)** People a busy building their lives upon lies the devil has fed their minds, that they have chosen to believe. **(promises all gives nothing) :13** Cheated: outwitted, deceived, swindled.

How did Satan get to her? Through the 5 physical senses and mind **(did not see Satan behind)** Paint false picture **(Eve was deceived wholly.)** Do not let anyone or any thing poison your mind. **I TIM 2:14** Deluded and fell into transgression, tricked become a wrong doer, yielding to deception.

ROM 8:6 For to be carnally minded is death. Separates from God's blessing. Right in heart, wrong in head. **II COR 11:2&3** Imagination be corrupted. Any means and any method. Subtle: 1/3 angels deceived. Con artist, phony as $3 or a wooden nickel, angel of light by His coming. Your minds corrupted, seduced from whole hearted, sincere, pure devotion to Christ. Your thought be led astray from a sincere and pure devotion. Corrupt: hucksterism. Embalmed with unbelief.

2 TIM 3:13 But evil men and seducers shall was worse deceiving and being deceived physiological warfare. Head game. The evidence of a corrupt mind is a tongue that produces death.

MATT 24:4 Take heed. Cares of life, deceit of wealth, lust of others. ***COL 2:8 Beware lest any man spoil you through philosophy and vain deceit.***

EPH 6:16 Fiery darts **HEB 12:3&4** Resisted unto blood. Direct your mind upon that which you want to become. **ISA 44:20** Worshipping on idle. A deluded mind has led him astray.

JER 17:9&10 Read Amplified. When did deceit enter into the heart of man?

HIGHWAY OF DELIVERANCE

NUM 12:1 Spike against, put down, belittled, debased, **(in their opinion had missed God)**

:2 By us? Just as good, if not better **(Absalom)**

:3 Meek above all = it is why God could use him.

PS 25:9 ***The meek will he guide in judgement: and the meek will he teach his way.***

MATT 5:5 ***Blessed are the meek: for they shall inherit the earth.***

:9 Anger of the Lord: hate, pride, haughty spirit

:10 Leprous.

PS 76:9 ***When God arose to judgement, to save all the meek of the earth.***

I TIM 6:11 ***But thou, O man of God, flee these things: and follow after righteousness, godliness, faith, love, patience, meekness.***

READ I KING 21:25-29

:25 Incited **(she was eaten by dogs)**

:26 Abominably.

:27 Heard words

:21-24 God's judgement

- **a.** Rent clothes
- **b.** Sackcloth
- **c.** Fasted
- **d.** Lay
- **e.** Softly

:29 Ahab humbled

PS 147:6*The Lord lifteth up the meek: he casteth the wicked down to the ground.*

II CHR 34:1 Josiah

:24&25 Judgement

:27 Heart **(care of problem)**
Tender, humble thyself, heard word.

Ren Clothes, weep

:18&19 Heard the Word
(Pharo hardened his heart)

II TIM 2:25*In meekness instructing those that oppose themselves; if God peradventure will give them repentance to the acknowledging of the truth.* (Jonah 3:3)

ISA 26:5*For he bringeth down them that dwell on high: the lofty city, he layeth it low; he layeth low, even to the ground; he bringeth it even to the dust.*

JON 3:3,4 Forty days

:5 Believed God. Fast, sackcloth

:6 Sat in ashes

:7 Not drink

:8 Cry mightily unto god turn everyone from his way, violence.

:10 Saw works, God did not.

GAL 6:1***Brethren, if a man be overtaken in a fault, ye which are spiritual, restore***

JAM 1:21 Lay apart all filthiness. Strip yourselves. Meekness: humble spirit.

JOB 42:6 wherefore I abhor **(myself)** and rent in dust and ashes.

PS 22:26***The meek shall eat and be satisfied. They shall praise the Lord that seek him: Your heart shall live forever.***

c:\advrsary\highway

DR. JEKYLL AND MR. HYDE

READ JAMES 3:10-12

(Perplexity) Duplication of life, dual natured, two personalities. **(Robert Lewis Stevenson-wrote Dr. Jekyll and Mr. Hyde)** Dr. Jekyll believed in duplication. He desired to separate these elements, managed to compound a drug by which one would dethrone the other found himself to be ten-fold more wicked. He lived a double life. Existence. Until wickedness took complete control. He committed suicide.

GEN 3:5 Serpent promised Adam equality with God. She drank of his cup. And what came forth has been the horror of man ever sense. A Mr. Hyde.

ROM 7:18-22 Frustration. *In my flesh **(bitter water, salt water)**

I JHN 2:16 Lust of the flesh, lust of the eyes, pride of life.

(Man lives a double life: good and evil) Whether in mind or actions. *Then Jesus came and said; drink from my cup and you will never be the same.

ROM 7:24&25*O wretched man that I am! who shall deliver me from the body of this death?I thank God through Jesus Christ our Lord. So then with the mind I myself serve.*

II COR 5:17*Therefore, if any man be in Christ, he is a new creature: old things are passed away*

JHN 15:5 I am the vine, ye are the branches, etc. Abram-Abraham, Sarai-Sarah. Jacob-Israel, Simon to Peter, John and James, to Sons of thunder, Saul-Paul.

READ GAL 5:16-25

I PET 2:11 *Dearly beloved, I beseech you as strangers and pilgrims – abstain from fleshly lusts, which war against the soul.*

*Whatever cup you drink from will depend who will be in control.

ROM 6:16*Know ye not, that to whom ye yield yourself to obey, his servants, ye are to whom ye yield yourself to obey, his servants, ye are to whom ye obey, whether of sin unto death, or of obedience unto righteousness.*

READ Rev 2:17

KIBROTHHATTAAVAH

(convince in great danger)

[I] **I PET 5:8** [amp] Poised to pounce. "Exercise self control, awake, alert.

*Wants to destroy our immortal soul, (knows His time short) Drag you to hell!

ISA 14:12 How art thou fallen from heaven, O Lucifier... EPH 6:12 For we wrestle... **JHN 10:10** The thief ***2 COR 10:3 For though we walk....***

Hot on our trail. Constantly interfering with God's plans. **I THES 2:18** Once and again Satan... **LU 22:31** Simon, Satan hath... (constantly asking -- Job) ***ECCL 2:1 My son if thou come to serve...***

2 COR 11:2

II **2 COR 11:2**. Chaste: holy, pure, sinless. **:3 I** fear {deeply concerned, sceptic} [1] Any means = devil wants to steal our commitment, love, heart away from God! Enemy is consumed with our destruction, obsessed, possessed with it! Can taste it. [2] Beguiled = "deceived, tricked, hoodwinked, hustled, fooled. **REV 12:19** Deceiveth the whole world. "deceive number in Bible" = Believe something hook, line and sinker! ***I COR 3:18 Let no man deceive himself...*** **JAM 1:22** But be ye... **I JHN 1:8 If we say....** ***GAL 6:3 For if a man think himself.... GAL 6:7 Be not deceived, God... EPH 4:14 That ye hence...*** **EPH 5:6 Let no man decieve you with vain... MAT 5:4** Jesus. = Take heed that no man.... ***I TIM 2:14 & Adam was not deceived, but...*** **COL 2:18 Let no man beguile you...** ***2 TIM 3:13 But evil men and seducers shall wax... I JHN 3:7 Little children, let no man deceive you: he that doeth...***
SUBTILITY = crafty, intelligent, outsmarts us, wisdom of world, = manipulates

I PET 2:18

III **2 PET 2:18**. Lust of flesh. ***JAM 1:13 Let no man....*** Wantonnes. ***EPH 2:3 Among whom also we all....*** **I JHN 2:16,17**. Lust of eyes, flesh, pride... ***ROM 6:16 Ye are the servants to whom ye obey.*** ***MATT 7:21 Not every one that saith unto me Lord, Lord.... 12:50** For who... Ex: Wagon going down him, no brakes...
{Utter arrogant nonsense and use physical cravings to lure into immorality} **:19** Slaves of corrupt habits rottenness! **:20** Escaped slum of sin.
2 TIM 2:1

IV **2 TIM 2:1-4**. (A fighting man) **:11** Dearly beloved, I beseech you as strangers and pilgrims, abstain from fleshly lust, which war against the soul. ***EPH 4:7 Neither give place to the devil....*** *Two battle lines [1] Sin within [2] Demonic without **I JHN 3:8** ***For this purpose as.... LU 4:18 Spirit of the Lord is.... ZEC 4:6 Not by might, nor power, but by....*** We must confront evil, not compromise. *Don't tolerate, pamper, play, games, change doesn't come easy.

2 COR 10:4&5

V **2 COR 10:4,5. REV 12:11** They overcame him... **JAM 4:7** Submit yourself therefore... ***PRO 11:9 Through knowledge.... LU 10:19 Behold I give unto... EPH 6:13 Wherefore take unto you the...*** **:14** Stand therefore having... ***2 TIM 3:16 All scripture is given ... 2 SAM 22:40 For thou hast girded me with***

strength to battle: them that rose up against me hast thou subdued under me. PS 44:83 Through thee will we push down our enemies, through thy name we will tread them under that rise up against us. MATT 16:18 Gates of hell shall not prevail.....

OBEDIENT SERVANT

DEUT 8:1,2 Observe to do **(James 1:22 be ye)**

JAM 2:21 ***Was not Abraham our Father justified by***

Live, multiply, possess.

:2 To humble, prove, know what's in thine heart

:3 Humbled, suffered thee to hunger

:5 Chastened

:16 Prove thee.

PHIL 4:11-13 ***Not that I speak in respect of want for I have learned,***

HEB 2:17,18 Suffered: felt the pain of temptation and trial. Succor: give immediate help, to run to the cry **(assist, relieve)** those who are being tempted, tested, tried.

HEB 4:12,14,15 All points tempted: tested in all respects, in every way **(devil did not let up for 33 1/2 years)** Yet remained without out sin.

:15 Touched: sympathize, fellow feeling.

Infirmities: our feeble flesh. **(Do not tolerate, pamper, pet ungodly things in your life)**

JHN 14:30 ***The prince of this world cometh, and hath nothing in me....***

MATT 6:13 ***Lead us not into temptation but deliver us from evil...***

MATT 26:41 Watch and pray that ye enter not into temptation: the spirit indeed is willing, but the flesh is weak.

ROM 6:16*Know ye not, that to whom ye yield yourselves* ...

EPH 4:27*Neither give place to the devil.*

HEB 5:6,7 Flesh: earthly life, clothed in humanity, a man on earth. Strong crying and tears: in desperate prayer and the agony of tears. Death: Grave In that: because He feared God, reverent submission.

:8 Learned. Found out from He suffered what it means to obey. *Through the pain which he underwent, the knowledge came to him of what it was to be under God's orders. **(Applied the Word)**

PHIL 2:8*Became obedient unto death, even the death of the cross.*

"NOT MY WILL BUT YOUR WILL"

PROV 11:9*Through knowledge shall the just be delivered.*

HEB 12:1-4 Witnesses: encircled, surrounded, on every side, vast crowd of spectators, **(others who have paid the price)** Lay aside: stripping off every encumbrance, throw off every impediment, hindrance. Easy beset: addition **(you have got to have it)** Entanglement, clings to us. Run: not walk. Patience: determination, made up mind perseverance, resolution.

:2 Despising: contempt, scorned its shame, caring nothing thinking nothing making light of its disgrace.

:3 Consider: think constantly, take your standard from him. Against: contradiction, opposition, bitter hostility. Wearied and faint: wearied, exhausted, get tired, give up. *Lose your purpose or courage.

:4 Striving against sin: struggled and fought agonizingly against sin.

PS 119:133*Let not any iniquity have dominion over me.*

Indulgence is the way of the flesh, discipline and order is

the way of the Spirit.

READ REV 22:1-5

DEVIL -- OVERRATED

(TEMPEST IN A TEAPOT)

Faith and Unbelief **(Head and Heart)** *Sea of Galilee, Storm.

ISA 14:9-17 **:13 & 14** 5 times the word I is mentioned **(selfishness opposite of Godliness)** check out your conversation! Who are you always talking about. Full of pride, puffed up. "Big talk" Hot air. Satanic syndrome.

EZEK 28:11-19 Ascend, exalt.

God doesn't have to boast! He is the author.

*All of creation shouts God's greatness and yet the devil seems like he steals God's thunder.

OBADIAH 4*Though thou exalt thyself as the eagle, and though thou set thy nest among the stars, thence will I bring thee down saith the Lord.*

We give the devil to much credit. **(Blow His trumpet.)**

II THES 2:3-4 So proudly insolently.

*Devil is out to tear down all that is Godly, holy, righteous, etc. And to exalt that is contrary to God's will, sickness, poverty, sin, evil. Lay it on thick. **(Belittles, makes light of God)** We swallow the devil's big lies, and won't believe God's simplest truths. "Man of old now the greatness of God and satan's insignificant against God.

REV 12:9 Deceiveth the whole world. And angels, **(seducer)** Devil is over rated. Deceived into thinking he is something. When next to God, he is nothing **(spirit of**

deception)

II COR 10:4&5 Every high thing **(lifted up)** Amplified.

Make a mountain of a mole hill.

Don't fall for the devil's bluff.

PS 99:5,9*Exalt ye the Lord our God.*

Do not undersell God.

*Meditation on problem, temptation, circumstances will enlarge it.

*Meditate on God's Word. Devil wants us to blow his trumpet.

PS 18:46*Let the God of my salvation by exalted.*

Laugh at his lies.

Give no place to the devil.

THE PIG IN THE MUCK

2 PETER 2:20-24

POLLUTIONS The vices of the ungodly which contaminates a person in his intercourse with the world.

READ GAL 5:19-21

ENTANGLED Involved.

READ JAMES 1:12-15

OVERCOME Subdue, conquer, prevail.

JHN 1:9*That was the true Light, which lighteth every man that cometh into the world.*

Through the knowledge of Jesus Christ. Why?

READ HEB 4:14-16

Don't run away from God, run to God.

READ HEB 2:17-18

SUCCOR A helper, a protector. Given as a title of a citizen in Athens, who had responsibility of seeing to the welfare of resident aliens who were without civic rights. We are aliens on earth.

I COR 10:13 Never going to be temptation you cannot overcome through Jesus. Have to realize that Your helpless without Jesus. And You can only depend on him.

*Temptation isn't sin, its when lust is conceived.

GAL 5:1 Christ has made us free. Bondage is sin and sin brings death.

How? Through Jesus.

II COR 10:4&5 **(Dunamos)** "Mighty" Able, strong, powerful.

Sin exalted itself against the knowledge of God. Bring every thought into line with God's Word.

And when you don't, that is when you get sad, depressed, confused, bewildered, and sin sets in.

REV 21:7 Overcomes, subdue, conquer, prevail, got the victory.

Do not let sin overcome you. You overcome sin through Jesus.

PURIFIED GOLD

I PET 1:3-9 HEB 5:8-9 II COR 12:9-10 JAMES 1:12-13
I PET 5:8-9

I PETER 1:3-9 Trial **(Faith)** Devil, see what your made out of "Pressure" *Get you to get out of faith. Squeeze, compression, pinch. Fire and pressure: will bring out the impurities! **(It isn't what comes to you that makes or breaks, but attitude)** Hold Satan in realm of Faith will whip Him every time! "Praise: Honor and Glory. *Abraham: strong in Faith. Example: Real flavor of tea comes out in hot water.

HEB 5:8-9 Obeyed God's Word above and over five senses.

Jesus: pressure, storm at sea, crowd at cliff, taxes, and death.

II COR 12:9-10 **Infirmities:** weakness and inability. Takes pleasure in them! Not for! If we believe and trust God, He can turn any situation around for us. Strong: powerful, capable, possible.

JAMES 1:12-13 Endure, remain, abide, continue, preserve.

(Through faith and patience) Fortitude. Do not bow you knees to the devil or His afflictions.

I PET 5:8-9 **Resist:** stand against, oppose. *In faith, afflictions and hardship. **(Many are the afflictions of the righteous etc.)**

SUBMITTED AND RESISTING

I PET 5:8&9 Your adversary. *When you submit to something you end up being filled, controlled, dominated by it.

READ JAM 4:7-10

Submit to who? sin, flesh, devil, world.

SUBMIT Surrender, conform, comply, obey, lamb like (spirit, soul, mind, body, mouth, emotions). Our sufficiency is of God, in his strength we gain the victory! God: mind, soul, body, spirit.

PS 91:4 His truth shall be thy shield and buckler.

EPH 6:10Finally, my brethren, be strong in the Lord and in the power of his might.

(LET GOD ARISE AND HIS ENEMIES BE SCATTERED)

ISA 26:3Thou wilt keep him in perfect peace, whose mind is stayed on thee.

GEN 6:22Thus did Noah according to all that God commanded him, so did he.

RESIST Military term, set oneself against, declare war, oppose, wage battle, stand firm, withstand. (Immediate, consistent, boldly, vigorously, unceasingly) Not delayed spasmodic. Passivity will kill you. (Cannot resist if not yielded)

HEB 12:3,4 Jesus prayed. Pray that you enter not into temptation. Indulgence is way of the flesh. Discipline and order way of the spirit!

EPH 6:11Take the whole armor of God, that ye may be able to stand against, wiles of the devil.

READ MATT 4:1-11

(To be tempted)

I JHN 2:16 Lust of flesh of eyes, pride of life.

:3 Lust of flesh

:4 Yielded to God

:6 Pride of life

:7 Yielded to God

:8&9 Lust of eyes

:10 Yielded to God

:11 Devil left, after resisted.

HEB 2:14 (Through death destroyed him that had the power of death)

A. Anointing
B. Position
C. Authority--responsibility

SUBMITTED AND RESISTING

I PET 5:8&9 Your adversary. *When you submit to something you end up being filled, controlled, dominated by it.

READ JAM 4:7-10

Submit to who? Sin, flesh, devil, world.

SUBMIT Surrender, conform, comply, and obey, lamb like **(spirit, soul, mind, body, mouth, emotions)**. Our sufficiency is of God, in his strength we gain the victory! **God:** mind, soul, body, spirit.

PS 91:4*His truth shall be thy shield and buckler.*

EPH 6:10*Finally, my brethren, be strong in the Lord and in the power of his might.*

(LET GOD ARISE AND HIS ENEMIES BE SCATTERED)

ISA 26:3*Thou wilt keep him in perfect peace, whose mind is stayed on thee.*

GEN 6:22*Thus did Noah according to all that God commanded him, so did he.*

RESIST Military term, set oneself against, declare war, oppose, wage battle, stand firm, withstand. **(Immediate, consistent, boldly, vigorously, unceasingly)** Not delayed spasmodic. Passivity will kill you. **(Cannot resist if not yielded)**

HEB 12:3,4 Jesus prayed. Pray that you enter not into temptation. Indulgence is way of the flesh. Discipline and order way of the spirit!

EPH 6:11 ***Take the whole armor of God, that ye may be able to stand against, wiles of the devil.***

READ MATT 4:1-11

(To be tempted)

I JHN 2:16 Lust of flesh of eyes, pride of life.

:3 Lust of flesh

:4 Yielded to God

:6 Pride of life

:7 Yielded to God

:8&9 Lust of eyes

:10 Yielded to God

:11 Devil left, after resisted.

HEB 2:14 **(Through death self destroyed him that had the power of death)**

- **A. Anointing**
- **B. Position**
- **C. Authority--responsibility**

SUBMIT & RESIST

JAMES 4:1-10 Instructions to Christians, fits in today's society. **2 TIM 3:16** ***All scripture is give by inspiration of God and is profitable for doctrine for reproof, for correction, for instruction in righteousness.*** 4:2 ***Preach the Word be instant***

in season, out of season: reprove, rebuke, exhort, with all long suffering and doctrine.

SUBMIT: Yield, surrender, comply, turn yourself over. **(:7) :6** Proud, do not yield.

To who? To sin. **PS 119:133** ***Let not any iniquity have dominion over me.***

ROM 6:14 ***For sin shall not have dominion over you.*** FLESH! ***ROM 8:4 Who walk not after the flesh but after the spirit. ROM 8:6 For to be carnally minded is death....*** INTELLECT! -- ***PRO 3:5 Trust in the Lord with all thine heart;....*** DEVIL **EPH 4:27** ***Neither give place to the devil.***

WORLD PS 1:1 ***Blessed is the man that walketh not in the counsel of the ungodly.***

CIRCUMSTANCES: ***2 COR 5:4 For we walk by faith, not by sight. Yielded, servant to...***

ROM 6:16 ***Know ye not, that to who ye yield yourself servants to obey, his servants ye are to whom ye obey; whether of sin unto death, or of obedience unto righteousness.***

Most Christians are slaves to their flesh, intellect, people, and circumstances. Do not move toward degradation but perfection. When you submit to something you end up being filled, controlled by that force.

The Lordship of Jesus will do you absolutely no good if you do not submit to it. Our source of victory, power, authority, and deliverance is not from the flesh, intellect or the world, but from God!

RESIST: Stand against, fight, attack, who? The devil. When? When or after you submit to God. The devil doesn't have to obey you if you're not submitted to God. Just squeeze tighter. You have to die to self and live unto God.

GAL 2:20 I live yet.

FLEE Run in stark terror. Devil is not terrified of us but of the **NAME AND AUTHORITY OF JESUS**

PS 44:83 ***Through thee will we push down our enemies, through thy name we will tread them under that rise up against us.***

I believe we have totally under estimated the authority we have in Jesus. His name represents complete and total authority and ability. The devil, sickness, poverty, ungodly thoughts cannot stand against the name of Jesus.

PROV 27:2 When the righteous are in authority, the people rejoice.

GEN 1:28 Subdue and have dominion. Over your life, home, Adam was to keep Garden free of satanic influence.

We must exercise authority. Take your place of authority. If you do not the devil will kill you!

SATAN

READ LUKE 4:1-14

SATAN Not a myth, abstract power, figment of imagination, boggy woggy. Superstition. He is mentioned 371 times in the Bible.

(Ignorant of Satan not ready for battle) Was Lucifer but committed high treason. "He is diametrically opposed to the three God Head."

(Cannot harm God so He destroys man.)

NAMES **Satan:** adversary or opposer. **Devil:** slander or accuser.

Wicked One: Source of wickedness, prime mover of all evil. Belial, worthless, reckless, and lawless.

Beelzebub, leader of evil spirits.

:1 Holy Ghost is essentially necessary

:3 Times temptation, tries to catch off guard **(strategically planned)**

READ I JHN 2:15-17

Lust of flesh, eyes, pride of life. **(Root of all sin is selfishness)**

:4 It is written **(weapon)** Faith **(shield)** never let mind become, slack, or careless in thinking. **(Cannot resist Devil into completely yielding to God)**

LOOSE COMMUNION WITH GOD!
LOOSE INTEREST IN WORD!

**Do no enter Satan's territory!!!

:6 Was His to give **(Eyes)** *Know why Jesus came
"Easy way out"

:8 Did not pet the devil. Sword and shield.

:9 Prove yourself **(life)** Sword and shield.

(Satan will brag on you. Tries to puff up your head.)

:14 Power of the Spirit. **(Weakest Christian can overcome)**

CHAPTER EIGHT

Offensive Weapons

To take the initiative by beginning to attack or act aggressively towards the opposition. "security forces took the offensive ten days ago" synonyms: launch an attack, begin to attack, attack first, strike the first blow "our fleet will take the offensive within the next 48 hours" Related to go on the offensive: take the offensive, goes on the offensive, took the offensive.

IN DUE SEASON!

MR 4:1 To teach **:2** Taught: Preached, instructed, declared, parables, stories. Why?

ROM 10:17 ***Faith cometh***

JHN 8:32 ***Ye shall know the truth***

PR 11:9 ***Through knowledge shall the just be delivered.***

I PET 2:2 ***As new born babes, desire milk.....***

EPH 4:14 ***That we henceforth be....***

ISA 28:9 Teach, understand? The weaned: not babies, infants, newborns, "breast fed" Ex: carry about, diapers, helpless **:10** Must be, precept.

MATT 7:25 Built upon a rock.

EPH 2:21 ***In whom all the building fitly framed*** **:11** Stammering: tongues (ACTS 2:4)

EPH 5:18 ***Be not drunk with wine*** **:12** The rest, refreshing Would not hear: believe, accept, receive.

MRK 4:3 Harken (listen, pay attention, absorb, give heed, drink in) **:14** Sows Word. *The incorruptible seed.

6 Responses #1 :15 Satan steals Word. Big trouble, totally vulnerable! **:16** Gladness, doing something #2 **:17** No roots, do not hold onto, depend, build, **:18** Hear the Word #3 **:19** Cares anxieties, worries, concerns of this time, age. Riches: false glamour of wealth. Lust: cravings of many things. Choke: smothers, no room, time, energy, finances left to be a doer.! Unfruitful: produce no crop.

I JHN 2:15&16 Lust of flesh, of eyes, pride of life. **:20** Good ground, rich soil. *Nothing wrong with he sun, oxygen, rain, temperature. *It is the soil! If only! No, the problem is you and me. Hear, receive, listen and take it in, welcome it, embrace it.

PS 1:2 But his delight is in the law. #4 Thirty fold. #5 Sixty fold. #6 Hundred fold **1:37** Mary. Let it be done to me according to thy Word!

LU 13:6-9 **:6** Man=God Vineyard: church Fig tree= You and I (Spirit) Sought: looking high and low, searching *None. **:7** Dresser: caretaker, husbandman, gardener. Behold: look, take notice, understand, seeking, expecting, hoping, anticipating. None. Why cumbereth: Suck out, nitrogen's from soil, sun, watch, atmosphere (environment not the problem) **:8** Dig -- turned up the soil. Dung: manure, fertilize. Let alone = mediator, stands in the gap.

PHIL 2:13 HEB 12:2 2 PET 3:18

SIN -- AN ACT OF DEATH

GEN 2:7 :18&19

Eden: delight, garden of abundance, blessings, provisions, Absolute declaration and evidence of God's love and commitment to man, what more could man went from God.

ROM 8:39*Nor height, nor depth, nor any other creature, shall be able to separate us from the love of God, which is in Christ Jesus our Lord.*

If not His provision, then definitely His sacrifice!

JHN 3:16*For God so loved the world....*

ROM 5:8*He commendeth his love toward us, in that, while we were yet sinners, Christ died for us.*

ROM 8:31&32*If God before us who can be against us? He that spared not his own Son...*

How shall He not with him also freely give us all things?

I JHN 4:10*Herein is love, not that we loved God, but that he loved us,and sent his Son to be the propitiation for our sins....*

I JHN 3:16*Hereby perceive we the love of God, because He laid down His life for us....*

I JHN 4:9*In this was manifested the love of God towards us because that God sent His only Son into the World that we might live through Him....*

GEN 2:16&17 Shall not! **Warning:** knowledge, understanding, perception. **Good:** becoming, agreeable to the flesh, desirable, seemingly beneficial to the flesh

(feels so good must be right)

EVIL Bad, a vicious disposition, calamity, malignant, misery, injury, to be broken, distress, pain, sorrow, morally wrong, worse then worst.

DIE Executed, perish, dying you shall die. "Clearly declared" Told it as it was! *Why? Loves us and wanted to create and I do not want you!

TREE OF SIN Not hurtful because forbidden, but forbidden because hurtful.

ROM 6:23 ***The wages of sin is death.***

Anything that is contrary to the will of God brings death.

GEN 3:1 **Subtle:** shrewd, crafty, sly. Yea, testing for gullibility. He entices her with the **(forbidden fruit of sin)** Major tool and No. 1 weapon of our enemy!

JHN 14:30 Hath nothing in me.

:3 **Midst:** sever, separate, set by itself.

LEST Devil at work diminished the finality of God's Word **(dare we take so lightly what God takes so severely)**

PROV 14:9 Fools make at mock of sin. **(Keep your distance)**

:4-6 **Saw:** consider, give attention, gaze intently, look upon. **Pleasant:** covet, crave, lust after, to be greedy. **Desire:** Take pleasure in may be attractive, but it kills. **Sin:** much more deep and damning in its results then we think. **Wise:** Insight, experience, prosperity, success. **(Was it? No, No, No.)** A lie, still is today.

:7&8 **Naked:** stripped, of righteousness, holiness, relationship, fellowship, intimacy. "Sin causes you to loose what God desires for you to possess" It perverts, twists, distorts our life. **Hid:** from before the face of God.

JAM 1:15*Then when lust hath conceived, it bringeth forth sin: and sin when it is finished bringeth forth death.*

:13 WHAT = How? Why? for what reason? (exclamation) "pain"

:16-19 Punishment, did God love any less? No, but did not make it ok! *Has God's opinion changed? No sin is sin no matter which side of Calvary. God hates sin. An abomination, disgusting, repulsive, revolting, shameful, hellish, deplorable, vile, foul, devilish, contemptible, rank, cursed, wretched, hideous, wicked, detestable, nauseating. **(It is contrary to everything that God is)** When we sin, we are spitting in the face of our blessed redeemer. (It is our enemy) a spiritual cancer!

I PET 2:11*Dearly beloved, I beseech you as strangers and pilgrims abstain from fleshly lusts, which war against the soul.*

Being born again does not give us a license to sin, but the ability to quite. **(Jesus came to set us free from sin, not live in it)** Woe be to us if we are playing footsies with sin.

GEN 3:24 Drove: Expel, cast out, drive away, divorce.

Sin drove us out of the blessings of God, provisions, abundance, blessings and it keep us out!

GEN 3:24 **Drove:** expel, cast out, drive away, divorce.

Sin drove us out of the blessings of God, provisions,

abundance, blessings and it keeps us out! Examples: Moses couldn't cross Jordan, Saul lost kingship.

PS 34:14*Depart from evil and do good: seek peace and pursue it.*

ROM 6:15*What then? Shall we sin because we are not under the Law, but under grace? God forbid.*

TIT 2:12*Teaching us that, denying ungodliness and worldly lust, ye should live soberly, righteously and godly, in this present world.*

TIT 2:14*Who gave himself for us, that he might redeem us from all iniquity and purify unto himself a peculiar people, zealous of good works.*

DELIVERANCE SUNDAY -- NUMBER 1

READ **LUKE 11:14-26**

:14 We are not demon conscious, devil chasers. Yet will not ignore the presence and operation of. Man had a problem **(spiritual)** Many trying to deal with outward, not inward! Outward is but tip of the iceberg of what is really going on in your life. Source, birthing place, origin, root cause was demonic. **(Disembodied spirit)**

Deranged both mind and body, destruction of your spirit, soul, and body. The conquest of satan demonic parasites, leaches, bloodsuckers, thieves and lives on peoples ungodly attitudes, thoughts, and imagination.

Can demons be in Christians? Yes, only in soul and body **(spirit no)** Example: Duane. *Behind every ungodly attitude, motive, word, action is a satanic influence, could be inhabitation, **(not possession)** only come forth as yield to it. Oppression, obsession, possession.

:20 **LUKE 4:18** Deliverance: set free from physical, mental and spiritual bondage. Cast out with his Word.

HEB 4:12 Surgery. Cutout Satanic tumors.

:21 Demons do everything they can to secure and fortify their hold on their **(old life). (II COR 10:4 and 5:21)**

Take the devil seriously. **JHN 10:10**

:22 **EPH 6:12** Wrestle, by force, hand to hand **(wrestling with body and etc)** Wherever Jesus is allowed to be Lord through commitment and obedience, Satan must go.

LU 10:19 Tread on serpents and scorpions

Real problem is passivity, must rise up in the Lord, resist, bind, and cast out.

II COR 10:4,5 Weapons of our warfare

PR 11:9 Through knowledge.

JHN 8:3 Truth sets us free.

God's Spirit can only minister deliverance to the degree you accept truth and act on it.

:23 **ROM 6:16**, ye are the servant to whom you obey. We are responsible for decisions, attitudes and actions of our lives.

HEB 12:15 Root of bitterness.

I TIM 6:10 Lose it and let go.

MATT 15:13 Every plant which my heavenly Father hath not planted, shall be rooted up eradicated, extracted, eliminated.

Don't tolerate, pet, pamper ungodly things in your life. Example: Seed grows to a tree. *Cycles: regularly recurring events being repented. **(Must want deliverance)** We are responsible to deal with what gave place to the devil.

:26 **EPH 4:27**. Place, give no opportunity, foothold, hand grip, loophole to Satan.

JAMES 4:7 Resist. Should be immediate, consistent, bodily, vigorously, unceasingly. *Unless the door has been closed, no permanent relief can be obtained. You have a tremendous amount to do with keeping free. Only way to stay delivered is through the application of truth.

PS 44:5*Through thee will we push down our enemies; through thy name will we tread them under that rise up against us....*

DELIVERANCE SUNDAY -- NUMBER 2

II SAM 11:1-5, 27, 12:12, II COR 10:3-5, II TIM 2:3&4, 4:6-8
I COR 4:8, I TIM 6:15, REV 5:10, 19:16

:1 We are kings.

Tarried: Ignored his duty, in activity breeds sin.

Old lazy thing. "go out and fight" **(self-centered, narrow minded people)** Indifferent, frozen chosen motionless. **(a decision not a feeling)** To serve God! Example: Stagnant water. Idle mind playground of devil! **(would never have gotten into the trouble He did)**

:2 Saw and continued looking. "gave place to the devil" lust conceived! **(This is when he sinned opend the door for destroyer to come in)**

READ

JAMES 1:13-15

Outcome is death. *You reap what you sow. *Fly a candle stick.

:6 Like going down a hill in wagon with no brakes, the longer you ride it the more dangerous it gets.

Look like He gets away with it.

12:11&12:14 Reaped death.

READ **II COR 10:3-5** and **11:3**

A spiritual warfare going on right now, out to destroy.

II TIM 2:4 **(I TIM 6:12)** Demands entire consecration. "Lay hold, grasp, seize, take possession of" "Devil is on the war path" Frustration, imitation, deception and affliction.

A loser in a Greek wrestling match had his eyes gorged out. The fight against demonic forces is no less desperate, serious or fateful! **(If your going to maintain and obtain your freedom, going to have to fight)**

PS 149:6*Let the high praises of God be in their mouth, and two edged savored in their hands.*

Entangled -- world, flesh, devil will lead you away from God. **(Caught up in)** It takes spiritual warfare to break spiritual bondage.

Entangled -- caught up in entwined, trapped, prisoner, *our choice.

EPH 6:10*Be strong in the Lord and in the power of His might.*

Way to please God. Must be an eager, active intense determination to live a life pleasing to God. **(A life and death struggle)**

READ

II TIM 4:6-8

I have fought and He (Paul) won through Jesus.

DELIVERANCE SUNDAY -- NUMBER 3

JHN 13:21-27 :1&2 12:3-6 I PETER 5:6-9 II COR 10:3-5

Jesus came to save us from the power of sin, dominion of Satan, damnation of hell.

JHN 13:27 Satan appears once in John. **(progressive take over)** Walked in and took over. Demons can inhabit the mind or of a Christian. **(Parasites)** Satan can only enter when you open the door. **(into His heart)** You are responsible for what you are, no one else, not a product of environment.

Behind every ungodly attitude, word action is a

satanic force. **(held accountable)** Do not be the devil's pawn or chest piece, puppet, tool, instrument. Judas kissed Jesus in order to betray Him. "Outward display" Inwardly self-centered. Say one thing and inwardly do another. *Judas loved Jesus, **(Jericho)**

I COR 10:12 ***Wherefore let him that thinketh he standeth take heed lest he fall.***

(Matt 10:1-8)

13:2 Had already betrayed Jesus in His heart. Before Satan entered into Him. Judas submitted to Satan's temptation.

I COR 10:13***There hath no temptation taken you such as is common....***

Birds over head, doesn't have to lay an egg in your hair. Devil wants you to defile, contaminate, pollute and corrupt yourself. "To be like him" In order for Satan to rule over you, you must open the door of your life by your own will.

EPH 4:27 No place, opportunity, foothold, hand grip, loophole. Satan enters a person where place is given to him. Master at ringing chimes.

We are responsible to deal with what gives place to the devil. He may have a foothold in your life, but only because we have given place to the devil.

ACTS 5:3 Ananias. We are responsible for the decisions, attitudes, and actions in our lives. We must pull out, root out, eliminate, extract, eradicate every ungodly root in order to void ourselves of demonic strongholds.

Do not tolerate the devil, pet, pamper, or listen to him.

JHN 12:3-6

CRITICAL ATTITUDE. (Watch out) Criticizer, fault finder, grumbler, murmurer, complainer. Do not tolerate, pet pamper, ungodly things in your life. Attitudes are reflective of motives. "Seed grows to a tree"

If you are not in the Word, guarantee into sin. **(Sin is like a soft bed, easy to get into, but very difficult to get out of.)** You have a tremendous amount to do with keeping yourself free, world, flesh, devil leads us away from God.

I PET 5:7-9

JAMES 4:7&8 Submit **(yield)** yourself therefore to God, resist the devil and he will flee from you. Submit: mind, body, mouth, shut and bolt the door to satan. Example: Three pigs. **(Let God arise and His enemies be scattered)**

Indulgence: way of flesh. Discipline and order way of the Spirit.

EPH 6:12

Knockdown, drag out fight. Conflict, collision course with Satan.

II COR 10:4&5

Our sufficiency is of God, in His strength, we gain the victory. In order to overcome and defeat our spiritual foe, we need to take advantage of all that God has provided. **Only way to stay delivered is through the application of the truth.**

EPH 6:11

STAND AGAINST. Military expression, take a fighting position.

PHIL 4:8*Finally, brethren, whatsoever things are true, honest just, pure, lovely, good report, if there by any virtue, praise think on these things.*

c:\advrsary\thatlife.wpd

THE TEFLON FACTOR

Involved in labratory of life **(tempted, tested, tried, tempered, proved)** If overcome, need to apply principles. Mold our lives, attitudes, behavior, conduct, reactions after Jesus.

I PET 2:21 A pattern: this kind of life, walk where Jesus did.

COL 3:1 ***If ye then be risen with Christ seek those*** .... Pattern role model.
:23 Not insult, attacked, mocked, accused, find fault, criticize, hated etc.
COL 3:12 ***Put on therefore, as ....*** **COL 3:13** ***Forbearing one another*** ....
I THES 5:15 ***See that none render evil for evil, unto any man; but ever follow*** ...
MATT 5:39 Other cheek. *How Jesus reacted? Bitterness, anger, hurt, world, flesh, devil, fly off the handle, Not but "love" Example: ancient legend: man on path, ugly creature, angelic messenger **(Samson) PRO 10:12** ***Hatred stirs old quarrels, but love overlooks insults.....*** **PRO 18:6** ***A fools lips enter into contention and mouth calleth for strokes....***

PRO 15:18 ***A wrathful man stirreth up strife: but he that is slow to anger appeaseth strife.*** **I PETER 3:8-12** Be tender, kind hearted, humble....
:9 Not insult, curse, abuse, called to bless. **:10** Enjoy life and see happy days.

ROM 12:20 ***Therefore in thine enemy hunger, feed him; if he thirst, give him drink, for in doing so thou shalt heap coals of fire on his head.....***

EPH 4:32 ***And be ye kind to one another....*** **(Keep a sweet, helpful, productive spirit)**

MATT 5:9 Blessed are the peacemakers: for they shall be called the children of God.

MATT 26:62-63 **JAMES 3:17,18** ***But the wisdom that is from above is first pure,***
:18 ***And the fruit of righteousness is sown in peace of them that make peace.***

27:13,14 Was not a pacifist, a time to speak, quiet.

__ISA 42:2__ ***He shall not not cry, nor lift up, nor cause his voice to be heard into the street.*** __ISA 53:7__ ***He was oppressed and he was afflicted, yet he*****.....** __ACTS 8:32__ ***Opened not his mouth: he is brought as a lamb to the slaughter and as a sheep before her shearers is dumb, so he opened not his mouth.***

Lamb: not snake = strike, bite, wound, poison, kill. Skunk: spray, big stink
Cat: Scratches, tortures victim Must know who we are and what!

LUKE 23:33-39 Kept saying forgive, forgive **(for self)**

ROM 12:14 ***Bless them which persecute you: bless and curse not....***

LU 6:28 ***Bless them that curse you, and pray for them which despitefully use you.***

ROM 14:19 ***Let us therefore follow after the things which make for peace....***

TEMPTATION

I PET 4:12&13 Satan can tempt but cannot force!

ROM 8:18 ***For I reckon that the sufferings of this present time are not be compared with the glory which shall be revealed in us.***

I PET 1:3-9 Manifold temptation **(trial of faith)** Devil wants to see what your made out of: pressure, squeeze, pinch. **(Wants to get you out of faith, spirit into flesh, hate, bitterness)**

Fire and pressure causes impurities to come to the surface!

*Hot water brings out real flavor tea, steak, potatoes. Faith brings praise, honor, and glory.

READ
JAMES 1:12-15

:12 Blessed, happy, well off, fortunate, to be envied. Endure: Steadfast, **(cursed is He who falls)** remains, abides, preserves, continues. Love causes faith to work. "Lack of love, yield to sin." Don't bow your knees to the devil or His afflictions.

:13 Not God!!!

MATT 4:3 Tempter came to Jesus

I THES 3:5 Tempter

1:2&3 Fall: surrounded. Praise God in the midst. **(Paul and Silas)**

:14 Drawn away: dragged forth.

Entice: Lure and bait (Not sin yet)
*We have to keep door closed to Satan.

:15 Conceived: clasp, capture, seize

Pro 1:10*My son, if sinners entice thee, consent thou not.*

Sin: is putting yourself before God, a desire to please your flesh against God's will. Example: Like wagon going downhill.

*House fell: Because had a weak foundation, storm did not create weakness in the structure, but revealed. Example: driver's test

II Pet 2:9*The Lord knoweth how to deliver the Godly out of temptations.*

THAT'S LIFE!

I PET 4:12,13 5:8-10 HEB 5:8-9 ACTS 14:19-22 II COR 12:9-10

I PET 4:12-13

Beloved: divinely loved ones. Strange: unusual, abnormal experience, extraordinary **(do not be shocked) (We are not immune to, exempt, free from suffering) HEB 11:32-39**

II COR 4:8*We are troubled on every side, yet not distressed!*

8:13 Rejoice.

ROM 8:18*For I reckon that the sufferings of this present time are not t o be compared with the glory which shall be revealed in us.*

PS 55:22*Cast thy burdens upon the Lord, and He shall sustain you.*

READ I PET 5:8-10

Don't be caught by surprise! Be prepared for a fight. **(monkey wrench, wind out of sails)**. Resist --- defy, oppose, challenge. *David against Goliath. Steadfast in faith. Hold Satan in the realm of faith will whip him every time. **(Devil will put tears in your eyes -- but God will put rainbow in your heart.)**

JHN 10:10*The thief cometh not, but for to steal, and to destroy....*

ACTS 10:38*How God anointed Jesus of Nazareth with*....

I JHN 3:8*For this purpose the Son of God was ....*

Afflictions: hardships, adversities, troubles, difficulties. Brothers undergo same troubles.

HEB 5:8,9 Learned how to apply the Word to do in every circumstance and situation.

Suffering isn't what teaches you!

(It is not what comes to you that makes or breaks you, but whether you apply God's Word or not)

PROV 11:9*Through knowledge shall the just be delivered!* (my people destroyed)

ACTS 14:19-22 Exhorting: urging, encourage **(continue in Faith)**

Tribulation: physical or mental hardships, adversities, problems caused by attacks from the world, flesh and devil! **(Many are the afflictions of the righteous but the Lord delivereth them out of them all.)**

Through -- by way of, passage **(kings highway)** Example: Giants in Canaan.

MATT 7:13 Straight and narrow = Greek root for tribulation **(hard, difficult, turbulent)**

PS 119:71 It is good for me that I have been afflicted. That I might learn thy states **(devil will give you a lot of opportunities to practice what you preach).**

II COR 12:9,10 Pleasure in, not for!

II COR 2:14*Now thanks be unto God which always causeth us to triumph....*

II TIM 4:18*And the Lord shall deliver me from every evil work and will preserve me unto his heavenly kingdom: to whom be glory for ever and ever, Amen.*

YOUR ADVERSARY THE DEVIL

Two opposing forces. God and devils. Light and darkness, good, and evil, positive and negative!

II COR 2:10,11 Advantage: Outsmart, upper hand, gain the ascendancy, do fraud! Not ignorant: blind, stupid, had winked, without perception. **(Amp: Wiles and intentions)**

*Satan can only take advantage of those who do not know their rights or won't exercise them.

HOS 4:6*My people are destroyed for lack of knowledge.*

ISA 5:13 Therefore my people have gone into captivity, because they have no knowledge. **(Ignorance and unbelief will open the door for Satan to kill you)**

Satan:

- **a.** Is not a myth.
- **b.** Does not have abstract power.
- **c.** Is not the figment of your imagination.
- **d.** Is not superstition, old wives tale, folklore, **(371 times)**

(Devil, Beelzebub, Abandon, Apollyon, Belial, old serpent, the dragon, wicked one, tempter, accuser of Brethren, adversary, God of this world, murder, thief, Father of lies, prince of darkness, enemies of God.)

ISA 14:12-17 **:13 & 14** Exalt my throne, my own God. Humanism, atheism, communism. **(Devil is always looking for a throne to sit on)**

:17 Wilderness, destroyed, prisoners.

JOB 1:7

I PET 5:8 Your adversary **(personal enemy)**

Seeking: Plotting, conniving, to bring about destruction.

Devour: Eat up, consume, wolf down. **(MAL 3:11)**

*Take the devil seriously, desires to destroy us, wants to cause our down fall! **(sober, vigilant)**

JHN 10:10 **Steal:** Rob, mug, plunder

Kill: Murder, slay, butcher, slaughter, psychopathic killer.

Destroy: Wipe out, obliterate.

*Would you accept candy from a man who was proven to be a psychopathic killer.

(Jesus is Life) (Devil is Death)

TURKEY ON THE LOOSE

Samson was born to bring deliverance, Spirit of God was on him, divine authority.

JUDGES 14:5 Roared against Him **(declaration of war)** ***Devil**.

PS 10:9 He lieth in wait secretly as a lion in His den; he lieth in wait to catch the poor; *Response? Fear, panic, passivity, or complacency.

:6 Spirit came mightily: attacked, do not sit around, rent.

PS 91:13 ***Thou shalt tread upon the Lion and the adder; the young lion and the dragon shalt thou trample under feet.*** **(Reward)**

:8 Honey in carcass

ROM 8:28 We know that all.

Reacted according to God's will!

GEN 45:5 Joseph: slavery, prison, saved Israel. Time and time again enemies defeated. **(Honey in carcass)**

READ
I SAM 17:34-36

Young man.

:35*I went after Him, I caught Him, "slew both" Let God arise and his enemies be scattered.* *Take the devil seriously.

JHN 10:10 Steel, rob, mug, plunder, kill, murder, slay, butcher, slaughter, psychopathic killer, destroy, wipe out obliterate.

II COR 11:3 By any means.

:25 Reward

I PET 5:8-9 Your adversary -- personnel, adversary, your conflict, walketh, roameth. Devil is a turkey, big old bird, running loose.

Seeking: Plotting, conniving, to bring about destruction.
Devour: Consume, wolf down, eat up. How?

Ignorance **(Hos 4:6)**
Unbelief
Disobedient
Rebellious

:9 Resist: stand against without wavering

READ **JAM 4:7-10**

Do not bow your knees
"Honey in carcass"

JAM 4:7 Submit yield, conform, comply, obey, **(spirit, soul, body, mouth, emotions)** In His strength, we gain the victory.

PS 91:4*His truth shall be thy shield and buckler.*...

EPH 6:10*Finally my brethren, be strong in the Lord and in the power of his might.*...

Resist: military term, set one's self against, declare war oppose, wage battle, stand firm, **(immediate, consistent, boldly, vigorously, unceasingly)**

*Not delayed, spasmodically, passivity will get you killed. Get the turkey and enjoy the meat.

CHAPTER NINE

Defensive Weapons

The Definition of defense is the act or action of defending, or protecting yourself. It is the capability of resisting attack. It is a means or method of defending or protecting oneself, one's team, or another; also : a defensive structure. It could also be a **Truth** in support or justification. In court it is the collected facts and legal methods used by a defendant to protect and defend against a plaintiff's action. In the military there are Weapons specifically used to overcome an attacking enemy!

***James 4:7 Submit yourselves therefore to God. Resist the devil, and he will flee from you.**

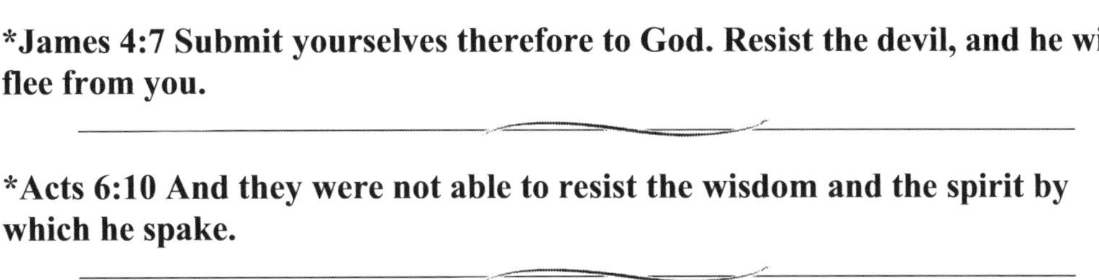

***Acts 6:10 And they were not able to resist the wisdom and the spirit by which he spake.**

***Hebrews 12:3 For consider him that endured such contradiction of sinners against himself, lest ye be wearied and faint in your minds.4 Ye have not yet resisted unto blood, striving against sin.**

***1 Corinthians 10:13 There hath no temptation taken you but such as is common to man: but God is faithful, who will not suffer you to be tempted above that ye are able; but will with the temptation also make a way to escape, that ye may be able to bear it.**

***Matthew 26:41 Watch and pray, that ye enter not into temptation: the spirit indeed is willing, but the flesh is weak.**

***James 1:12 Blessed is the man that endureth temptation: for when he is tried, he shall receive the crown of life, which the Lord hath promised to them that love him.**

***2 Peter 2:9 The Lord knoweth how to deliver the godly out of temptations, and to reserve the unjust unto the day of judgment to be punished:**

***1 Peter 5:8 Be sober, be vigilant; because your adversary the devil, as a roaring lion, walketh about, seeking whom he may devour:9 Whom resist stedfast in the faith, knowing that the same afflictions are accomplished in your brethren that are in the world.**

***Ephesians 4:27 Neither give place to the devil.**

***Ephesians 5:21 Submitting yourselves one to another in the fear of God.**

***Psalm 66:3 Say unto God, How terrible art thou in thy works! through the greatness of thy power shall thine enemies submit themselves unto thee.**

***Psalm 32:5 I acknowledge my sin unto thee, and mine iniquity have I not hid. I said, I will confess my transgressions unto the Lord; and thou forgavest the iniquity of my sin. Selah.**

SPIRITUAL WARFARE

EPH 6:10-12 JOHN 10:10 I PETER 5:8 II TIM 2:3&4 GAL 5:1

EPH 6:12 For **we: (Christian)** Against flesh and blood "Man is not our enemy."

Yes, **(Satan gets to us through people and circumstances)**

There is a spiritual warfare going on right this moment! The demonic world is out to destroy everything that it can.

JOHN 10:10 Steal, kill, destroy. **(Cannot harm God -- So destroys Man)**

Satan can only destroy where ignorance lies: sin or unbelief is! **(Jesus came to give us life)**

I PETER 5:8 Walketh about seeking whom he may devour! Cannot devour people who are walking in God's divine will and **WORD**! **(Cannot resist Satan until we are completely yielded to God.)**

Trap: Ensnare, devour. Try to lead you away from Gods will by lust of flesh, lust of eyes, pride of life.

II TIM 2:4 Warreth, entanglement **(caught up in)**. We are soldiers.

EPH 6:10&11 Be strong in God. Power of His might.

God has equipped us with:

- **a)** Authority: Jesus
- **b)** Power: Word
- **c)** Ability: Holy Ghost

PUT ON THE WHOLE ARMOR OF GOD AND STAND.

BRIDGE OVER TROUBLED WATERS NUMBER 1

MATT 18:20 Gathered not:

- **a.** Nationality
- **b.** Color
- **c.** Denomination
- **d.** Tradition
- **e.** Natural man

"But Jesus" *Not accident, by chance, but divine destiny, heaven purpose.

READ I ROM 5:6-10

Reconciliation **(important part)** Two types, 1st kind? Bad news and good news.

:6 Without: powerless, helpless, Spirit disabled, no way of escape **(from what?)**

SIN All have sinned, created a wall, barrier, impassable chasm between God and man.

JUDGEMENT Wrath, chastisement punishment for God.

Good news: due time appointed, 100 percent pure Love.

:8 Commendeth: revealed, expressed, demonstrated gave evidence, proof of His Love **(God reaching out today)**

JHN 3:16 God so loved the world that He gave His only Son proving that love reaches out to those who do not or deserve it. Still in rebellion, ungodliness, sin.

:9 Justified: pronounced righteous, acquitted by His blood, not goodness.

:10 Reconciled: Make peace, friends, win back, **(bring into a state of health, wholeness and spirit harmony through or by means of divine mercy or to bring change by means of divine mercy.)** A change in heart, purpose, priorities, life. *Made God's friends by believing in the redemptive work of God's son. His death has become a bridge to the Heavenly Father, divine connection.

EPH 5 Bone of his bone etc. Born of incorruptible, born again. Family: community of believers, kinship, brothers and sisters.

I COR 10:17***For we being many are one bread and one body: for we are all partakers of that one bread.***

COL 1:20 Blood

REV 12:11 Overcame. Reconcile to win back into union of relationship, etc. *Cleared a pathway, built a bridge, a way to the Father.

:22 Presented us faultless, blameless, innocent in His presence.

II COR 5:17 New person, in new world, new life begun, old finished, gone, everything, new and fresh, **(slate wiped clean)**

:18 Reconciled. Given: appoint, charge, commission bestow. Ministry: Office **(Five Fold)** Second reconciliation is making peace, friends, of healing, comfort, exhortation, love, forgiveness, mercy.

JHN 13:35 By this shall all men know... Called us to bless each other *build bridges. Not build walls, barriers, dividers, patrician's, but to pull down.

MATT 5:9 Blessed are the peace makers: for they shall be called the children of God. **(Peace Makers, appeasers, mediators)**

I PET 4:8 And above all things have fervent charity among ourselves: for charity shall cover the multitude of sins. *Cover: hide, veil, hinders the knowledge of. Bundle.

COL 2:2 Knitted together in love. *God has designed us to be eternally committed, connected, and obligated.

:19 WIT: proclaim, tell, Word: Message, ordained to speak.

:20 Paul: Pray, implore, beg, entreat get right with God.

BRIDGE OVER TROUBLED WATERS -- NUMBER 2

EPH 3:8-10 Church might now be used to display the innumerable aspects of God's wisdom. **(God raised up His church to reveal SELF)** "Mystery of Ages"

PS 133:1-3 **Good:** Pleasant, agreeable, excellent, valuable, prosperous, right and ethical. PLEASANT: Delightful, sweet, lovely, beautiful.

Dwell: Inhabit, abide, worship, endure, marry, eternally committed, connected, obligated.

ROM 12:5 ***So we being many are one body in Christ and every one members of one of another....***

:3 Commanded: appointed, ordained. Blessing: prosperity. Life: revival and renewal.

Unity in: One in hopes, dreams, aspirations, vision, purpose.

JHN 10:10 Steal, kill destroy unity.

MR 10:9 ***What God hath joined together, let not man put asunder ..*** Satan wants to separate, split, divide in order to conquer us.

JER 23:1 ***Woe be unto the pastors that destroy and scatter the sheep of my pasture, saith the Lord.***

JAM 4:11 ***Speak not evil one of another brethren.***

JUD 20:11 War against Benjamites **(raped and killed wife of a Levite)** were united! Knit: joined, compacted.

COL 2:2 Knit together in love.

I PET 3:8 Finally be ye of one mind: mobilized, banded and grouped together. *Need me and you to fulfill God's will.

NEM 4:16-21 Enemy sought to stop. Cause division. To rebuild needed team work, cooperation, participation **(mutual assistance)**

LUKE 9:1-6 Together, team, multiple ministry, **(Building the kingdom)**

FOR THE WORD SAKE

MR 4:3,14 The word

:26 Seed and word rise night and day!

:28 First blade, ear, full corn = progressive advancement **(must protect)**

:30, 31 When it is sown **(less than least),** world does not invest or put much hope in God's Word!

:32 Sown into soil: heart greater then all herbs.

ECCL 11:16 **:4** Observeth wind not sow, clouds not reap **(moved by circumstances)**

:5 Knoweth not

:6 In morning sow, evening give...

:15 Satan cometh "Robs the important in their life.

:16 Gladness **(sinks in will produce joy)**

:17 No depth, shallow, "only good time deep, convenient" **(not dependent upon, meat and potatoes)** A fad!

:18-19 Cares, riches, lust of things

God never meant for us to be under control of world flesh devil!

:20 Good grown

:24 More given "yielded"

PS 22:26The meek will he guide in judgement and the meek will teach his way.

READ I JHN 2:16

HEB 12:1 ***Let us lay aside the sin ...***

Temptations of Jesus in wilderness.

EPH 6:12***For we wrestle not against flesh and blood,....***

THE WORLD, THE FLESH, AND THE DEVIL

MR 6: 7-13 I JHN 2:15-16 MR 4: 2-8 MT 4:4-11 REV 19:11-16

MR 6:7 Power, "do we?" *Shout yes.

:8 Take nothing

(Many people want what they do not need and need what they do not want)

Staff only -- "Will provide everything else" El Shaddi not El Cheapo.

:12 Went out **(preached, cast out devils and healed sick)** "Some people like vultures only come to church when someone dies"

READ

I JHN 2:15-16

*World, flesh, devil will lead you away from God!

a. **Lust, flesh**
b. **Lust, eyes**
c. **Pride, life like a soft bed.**

Easy to get into but hard to get out of.

READ

MR 4:2-8

Yielded no fruit.

:18&19 **a.** Cares
b. Riches
c. Lust

*Satan is master at ringing peoples chimes

***(Word from sin or sin from WORD)**
"If your not in the **WORD -- YOUR IN SIN**"

*Some folk for everything, because they stand for nothing.
(Lie down with the pigs you will get up with the worms.)

MATT 4:3-11 **:4** Don't grumble, you do not have what you want. Praise God. You do not have what you deserve.

:11 Servant of whom you obey!

Angels minister to you when you stand.

READ **REV 19:11-16**

THE FOOLISHNESS OF WRATH

READ **MATT 2:1-18**

Wiseman.

a. **Forsook**
b. **Followed**
c. **Searched**
d. **Suffered**
e. **Discovered**

:3 Troubled: greatly agitated, deeply disturbed, upset, a bit angry. Why?

a. **Contrary to his plan**
b. **Under pressure**
c. **Impatient**
d. **Frustrated**
e. **Confused**

*Little things set people off. **(Not nature of God)** Example: Land minds. Major sign of end.

READ

GEN 6:11-13

I COR 3:3*For are ye yet carnal: for whereas there is ....*

PRO 29:22*An angry man stirreth up strife, and furious man aboundth in transgressions....*

JAM 1:20*For the wrath of man worketh not the....*

ECCL 7:9*Anger resteth in the bossom of fools.....*

:11 Wiseman in the presence of Christ **(Herod in palace-prison-cooking-tormented, angry)**

:12 Another way.

JAM 3 Fruit of righteousness sown in **(divinely inspired)**

PR 15:1*A soft answer turneth away wrath....*

PS 37:8*Cease from anger and forsake wrath.....*

:16 Mocked: outwitted, insulted,
(wiseman not manipulated)

Exceeding wroth: furiously angry, enraged. "Unchecked emotion -- not manliness" *Anger is seed of murder, dasterdly deeds! Example: Cain, Saul trying to kill Jonathan. Example: Moses struck the rock, Sons of Jacob against Joseph! Slaughtered in 10-mile radious.

:14 Departed into Egypt.

:19-21 Land of Israel. *Could come back, Herod was dead! Christ **(The Anointed One)** cannot move to a great extent in our lives until we deal a death blow to Herod.

COL 3:8*But now ye also put off all these anger, wrath, malice.....*

EPH 4:31*Let all bitterness and wrath and anger, and ....*

EPH 4:26*Be ye angry, and sin not:....*

:27*Neither give place to the devil....*

ANOINTING - OUT LINES

ALL THINGS POSSIBLE

GAL 3:5, I JHN 5: 13, 14 & 15, I JHN 3:22, MR 9:17-27, MR 11:22, 14

GAL 3:5 Miracles an event, action that apparently contradicts known scientific Laws, extraordinary, supernatural in origin and character. *{Something you need to happen that is beyond you present ability or resources} I need some miracles.

ACTS 6:6-8 **GAL 3:5** He -- whosoever, miracles by faith.

ACTS 6:8 Steven, full of faith and power, did great wonders and miracles among the people. Greatest demand. 5 absolutes. [1] Must know the will of God.

1 JHN 5:14&15

[II] **1 JOHN 5:14 & 15**. Confidence, anything, His will. [2] Plug into God

JHN 15:7, if ye abide in me, and my Word in You. [3] **WORD.**

ROM 10:17, Faith cometh by hearing etc.

[III] **I JHN 5:13** Written that you may believe.

[IV] [4] Praying in Spirit -- **JUDE 20** [5] Do, obey, put to practice,

JAM 1:22.
*Use shield of faith against temptations!

1 JHN 3:22

[V] **I JHN 3:22** Because, keep *Christianity is demonstration of the righteousness of God. {Takes faith to not Sin}

2 COR 10:4&5 ***Weapons of our warfare...***

EPH 6:16 ***Above all, taking shield of faith, where with ye...*** *Faith is a major protection against devil, sickness etc. Satan wants to rob our faith (confidence, trust, hope, commitment) by --- worldly, devilish, earthly things. Ex: **HEB 11** Woe to the devil if we ever get serious with God. Satan wants to fill our minds with doubt, to steal our precious faith.

I PET 1:7 ***That the trial of your faith being much more precious than of gold, that perisheth, though it be tried with fire, might be found unto praise and honor and glory at the appearing of Jesus Christ.***

HEB 12:2 ***Looking unto Jesus the author and finisher of faith.***

MRK 11:22

[VI] **MR 9:17-27**. **:18** Brags and boast **:21** How long? **:22** Boast **:19** Faithless generation (We limit Holy One of Israel) **:23** Art able, whatsoever things, (We limit God) Everything is possible for the one who has faith "in Jesus" **:25** Rebuked by saying = Rebuke and will loose you. Charge = command

MR 11:22

[VII] **MRK 11:22 [:14]** Faith of God {confidence} **:23** As many as -- say, move it, = calls by name. And does not waver, no inward doubts, hesitate. Believe -- persuaded, confident. **:24** Come to be, fulfilled.

YOUR CONFESSION IS THE EXPRESSION OF WHAT YOU BELIEVE. GOD HAS NEVER DONE ANYTHING WITHOUT SAYING IT FIRST.

ANOINTED VESSELS

ISA 64:8, JER 18:2-6, 2 KINGS 2:18-15

Our divine purpose, objective, Master's plan. A deep mysterious plan. ***I COR 2:9* eyes have not seen**. **Once we get a glimpse -- will motivate, compel, drive us on, energize us.

ISA 64:8 Clay - reddish mud, slime, mire.

JAMES 4:7 ***Submit yourself.*** **GEN 2:7** We are the dust of the earth. Without the potter's touch, that's all you will ever be compared to what you could be. **Potter** - He forms, fashions, shapes, molds, according to the purpose He has in mind for you.

** God is totally committed to the success of His product. Work - Hand - What God has called you to be cannot be done without His hands.

PHIL 1:6 ***Being confident of this...***

JER 18:1-6 **:3.** Wrought a work. We are on the wheel. **Marred** = **:4** to stiff, dry, a stone. What the potter can do with you is determined by what you are made out of.

2 TIM 2:20,21 But in a great way, God wants us to soar like eagles, but many Christians are content to scratch like chickens. **Rework** = Add water (spirit)! Does what He can!

2 KINGS 2:8 Elijah - 1) Mighty 2) Jehovah **Mantle** = Anointing.

ACTS 10:38 You know of Jesus.

I JHN 3:8

LU 4:18 {always used supernatural to shape people}

:9 Ask - **First** a) heard the call, b) forsook, c) followed, d) served, e) refused to turn back. **Saw** = **:10-12** Had a revelation of God, His man and His plan.

ACTS 7:55. Stephen saw glory of God, and Jesus on right side. **Rent clothes:** His old life, ideas, plans, entered a new realm, up to this moment a spectator! **A man at his best, apart from God, is but a weakling.

:13 Mantle = you will take a hold of the anointing. Step into the cloak of the anointing. **:9** double.

JHN 14:12 The works that I do before this a normal man.

2 COR 4:7 ***But we have this treasure in earthen vessels, that the excellency of the power may be of God and not of us.*** The anointing that flowing through Jesus now flow through us. It is the source, origin, essence of our success in fulfilling our purpose.

HEB 11:34,35 ***Who subdued kingdoms....***

BLOOD, FIRE, AND VAPOR THE MIGHTY HAND OF GOD

ACTS 2:14-21 :16

ACTS 2:14-21 That which = NOW, this moment, until return of Christ to earth. [1] **Filled with Spirit** = controlled, moved, overflowing, set a flame, {Something happens when Spirit and filled} **:15** Not drunken -- Looked drunk, intoxicated. [2] **Supernatural abilities** = gifts of Holy Ghost, unctions. [3] **Visions**. Dreams, divine insight Peter, Paul, John. [4] Signs **:19, 20** [5] Salvation. *Last day's, not only, technology break through, natural advances. But supernatural. ***ISA 40:5 & the glory of the Lord shall be revealed and all flesh shall see it together for the mouth of the Lord hath spoken it.*** [Much of it God -- some of it devil] **Must** = Not be paranoid. Ex: = Tongues of devil. ***2 TIM 1:7 God has not given a spirit of fear but of a sound mind***. *3 major points

[I] **I JHN 4:1** ***Beloved believer not every spirit, but try out...*** **:2** Jesus came in flesh "should have inner witness, not our heads" Carnal mind cannot understand! Not contradict, word, or nature! {Earthly ministry -- Pharisees, Sadducees, adamant man of Word! They declared Jesus, was of devil! Not lined up with their interpretation scriptures. [Contradicted laws of Leviticus, picked food, and healed and had people work on Sabbath day--Trinity]. *Absolute, outright, arbitrary disobedience -- in their understanding.* (He was wrong or they were) Ex: Same today. Seduction of Christianity! Wrong spirit. Wanted to kill Jesus, disciples -- no love, burn at stake.

2 TIM 3:1 Perilous days. **:5** Form of Godliness, denying = strangers to God's power.

I THES 5:19 **Quench not the Spirit** = Do not stifle what God is doing. **:20**

Prophesying **__:21__** Prove all things = test, hold fast = retain only what is good. *[Don't make a big deal].

III **Bottom line** = Changed lives, fruit of the spirit and people being saved.

ACTS 4:29

ACTS 4:29:30 Thine hand = signs, wonders, miracles. [They asked - we asked] Why? Multitudes got saved. **__:31__** Shaken = moved violently, rocked to and fro **__:33__** Got power **__5:12__** By the hands = signs, wonders.

LUKE 4:18 Anointed = divine impartation by the laying on of hands. **__I TIM 4:14__** ***Neglect not the gift that is in thee . . .*** ***__2 TIM 1:6__ Wherefore I put thee etc.*** The same miracle working power that was in Jesus and his hands is in us!

__LUK 10:19__ ***Behold I give unto you power ....*** ***__ACTS 11:21__ The hand of the Lord was with them; a great number believed and turned unto the Lord.***

DEUT 26:7

__DEUT 26:7,8,9__. ***__I PET 5:6__ Humble yourselves therefore under the mighty hand of God; that he may exalt you in due time!***

EXO 8:5

EXO 8:5 Your hand. **__9:22__** Your hand = creative ability, skill, talent, craftsmanship.

__:33__ Got power **__5:12__** By the hands = signs, wonders. ***__2 SAM 22:35__ He teacheth my hands to war so that a bow of steel is broken by mine arms.***

BLOOD, FIRE, AND VAPOR
THE MIGHTY HAND OF GOD

ACTS 2:14-21 :16 That which = NOW, this moment, until return of Christ to earth.

1.

:15 Not drunken -- Looked drunk, intoxicated.

2. Supernatural abilities = Gifts of Holy Ghost, unctions.

3. Visions, dreams, divine insight Peter, Paul, John.

4. Signs = :19, 20

5. Salvation

Last day's, not only, technology break through, natural advances. But supernatural Isa 40:5 & the glory of the Lord shall be revealed and all flesh shall see it together for the mouth of the Lord hath spoken it. [Much of it God -- Some of it Devil]

MUST Not be paranoid. Examples = Tongues of devil.

3 Major Points A. I Jhn 4:1 Beloved believer not every spirit, but try out... :2 Jesus came in flesh "should have inner witness, not our heads" Carnal, mind cannot understand!

B. Not contradict, word, or nature! {Earthly ministry -- pharisees, sadducees, adamant man of Word! They declared Jesus, was of devil! Not lined up with their interpretation scriptures.

[Contradict laws of Leviticus, picked food, and healed and had people work on Sabbath day--Trinity. *Absolute, outright, arbitrary disobedience -- in their understanding. He was wrong or they were) Example: Same today =
Seduction of Christianity! Wrong Spirit. Wanted to kill Jesus, disciples -- no Love, burn at stake., 2 Tim 3:1 perilous days.

:5 Form of Godliness, denying = strangers to God's power.

I Thes 5:19 Quench not the Spirit = Do not stifle what God is doing.

:20 Prophesying

:21 Prove all things = test, hold fast = retain only what is good. Do not make a big deal.

Acts 4:29 Bottom line = Changed lives, fruit of the spirit and people being saved.

Acts 4:29:30 Thine hand = signs, wonders, miracles.
[They asked - we asked] Why? Multitudes got saved.

:31 Shaken = moved violently, rocked to and fro

:33 Got power

5:12 By the hands = signs, wonders.

Lu 4:18 Anointed = divine impartation by the laying on of hands.

I Tim 4:14 Neglect not the gift that is in thee

2 Tim 1:6 Wherefore I put thee etc. The same miracleworking power that was in Jesus and his hands is in us!

Lu 10:19 Behold I give unto you power Acts 11:21
& Deut 26:7. The hand of the Lord was with them; a great number believed and turned unto the Lord. Deut 26:7,8,9

I Peter 5:6 Humble yourselves therefore under the mighty hand of God; that he may exalt you in due time! Exo 8:5

Exodus 8:5 Your hand. 9:22 Your hand = creative ability, skill, talent, craftsmanship.

2 Sam 22:35 He teacheth my hands to war so that abow of steel is broken by mine arms.

LOOSED FROM BONDAGE

I **ISA 58:6** Fasting and prayer -- You bring your spirit and body under authority of your spirit, through prayer and fasting.

II In bondage. **(ISA 5:13) (MR 5:1-5** A prisoner of Satan) Whom Satan hath bound. No man is free who is a slave to the flesh. Devil wants to put you in bondage, corrupt, defile, contaminate us. Sin is like a soft bed, easy to get in, hard to get out. **PS 102:20** God hears the groaning of the prisoners. Different kinds of prisons: bondage and captivity. ***PR 5:22 His own iniquities shall take the wicked himself and He shall be holden with the cords of his sin. 2 TIM 2:26 That they may recover themselves out of the snare of the devil who are taken captively him at his will.*** Source -- Birthing place -- origin root cause is demonic.

PS 146:5-10

III **ANOINTING**. Destroy, break, melt, set free, unbind, release, liberate). Burden removing yoke destroying power of God. Let God arise and his enemies be scattered. ***ISA 61:1 Proclaim liberty to the captives.*** **LUK 4:18** Deliverance to captives. ***2 COR 3:17 Now the Lord is that Spirit. Where the Spirit of the Lord is, there is liberty. ISA 10:27 Destroyed because of anointing. PROV 11:9 Through knowledge shall the just be delivered. JHN 8:32 Ye shall know the truth and the truth shall make you free. ROM 8:2 For the law of the Spirit of Life in Christ Jesus has made me from the law of sin and death.*** ***ISA 42:5-8**

MAT 16:18,19. Bind and Loose. Shall not hold out against her forbid. Bind and loose (keys). Gates of hell no prevail. ***DEUT 28:7 The Lord shall cause then enemies that up against thee to be smitten before thy face, they shall come out against thee one way and flee before thee seven ways. JHN 8:36 If the Son therefore shall make you free you shall be free indeed.*** **1 JHN 3:8** Destroy (loose)

ISA 59:19** Lift up a standard. ***I COR 4:20 For the kingdom of God is not in word but in power. I COR 2:5 Our faith should not stand in the wisdom of men but in the power of God. **ECCL 8:4** Where the Word of a king is there is power.
EPH 4:8
***EPH 4:8** He led captivity captive, (captives into captivity) prisoners.

V **FREEDOM**. No word was ever spoken that has held out greater hope, demanded greater sacrifice, ever came closer to being God's will on earth. True freedom is only found in God.

RELEASING THE POWER OF GOD
POINT OF CONTACT

GEN 1:1-3, ROM 12:3, MARK 5:25-30

GEN 1:1-3 Nine times (God says) Filled with faith "calls those things" Holy Spirit moved when God spoke faith. Gehazi saw. (already existed) "Every one saved at Calvary"

Faith plus Word -- Faith? 1) Link between natural and spiritual. **2)** Product of God from heart. **3)** Its the meeting ground between limited man to limitless God.**4)** Invisible hand bring spiritual into physical. **5)** Only pleases God. **6)** Simply believing what God says -- Speaking and acting.

Holy Spirit is hovering over us. Word with Faith (Faith gives substance) **ROM 12:3** Is dealt-given and measured from God. "It isn't enough just to have faith" Has to be turned loose, use it, released.

MRK 5:25-30 :34 Her faith released power. 1) She said 2) **:28** Image of seeing and feeling (hope) 3) Establish point of contact to release to release faith.

CONTACT -- Set action and time where you release your **FAITH**. Anything that helps you to come to a climax in your faith and release it to God.

It focuses your faith on God. (magnifying glass) Ex: runner and a gun fire. "Its expectancy" **:28** If I may but touch His clothes.

(All power has a point at which you make contact). A car -- light switch -- Source is connected to load. Unable to release your faith without point of contact. Might be -- hands -- oil --Word of God. Ex: myself -- centurion. Set time for releasing your faith -- Turn Loose will put Holy Spirit to work. (women touch cloak -- flowed) Capacitor-horse-jet.

You reach God by establishing a point of contact, releases power.

Ex: Moses and Red, Shout & Jericho, David and Slingshot, Peter's Shadow, Samson and hair, Mary and Word, Centurion and Word, Jesus and Word, Peter and come, Simon's mother and touch, Leper and Word, palsy and act on Word, handkerchiefs and aprons.

1) Say the Word 2) See yourself free 3) Establish point of contact 4) Act on it 5) Release your faith A) Heard 6) Receive your healing **GOD'S TIME IS ALWAYS THE NOW!**

CHAPTER TEN

Adversity

2 Corinthians 4:8-9 - [We are] troubled on every side, yet not distressed; [we are] perplexed, but not in despair;

Philippians 4:12-13 - I know both how to be abased, and I know how to abound: everywhere and in all things I am instructed both to be full and to be hungry, both to abound and to suffer need.

Proverbs 24:10 - [If] thou faint in the day of adversity, thy strength [is] small.

1 Peter 5:10 - But the God of all grace, who hath called us unto his eternal glory by Christ Jesus, after that ye have suffered a while, make you perfect, stablish, strengthen, settle [you].

2 Corinthians 12:9 - And he said unto me, My grace is sufficient for thee: for my strength is made perfect in weakness. Most gladly therefore will I rather glory in my infirmities, that the power of Christ may rest upon me.

Romans 8:28 - And we know that all things work together for good to them that love God, to them who are the called according to [his] purpose.

Joshua 1:9 - Have not I commanded thee? Be strong and of a good courage; be not afraid, neither be thou dismayed: for the LORD thy God [is] with thee whithersoever thou goest.

2 Chronicles 15:7 - Be ye strong therefore, and let not your hands be weak:

for your work shall be rewarded.

Romans 12:2 - And be not conformed to this world: but be ye transformed by the renewing of your mind, that ye may prove what [is] that good, and acceptable, and perfect, will of God.

Revelation 21:4 - And God shall wipe away all tears from their eyes; and there shall be no more death, neither sorrow, nor crying, neither shall there be any more pain: for the former things are passed away.

Psalms 34:19 - Many [are] the afflictions of the righteous: but the LORD delivereth him out of them all.

---

1 Peter 4:12-13 - Beloved, think it not strange concerning the fiery trial which is to try you, as though some strange thing happened unto you:

---

2 Corinthians 1:4 - Who comforteth us in all our tribulation, that we may be able to comfort them which are in any trouble, by the comfort wherewith we ourselves are comforted of God.

DOING THE IMPOSSIBLE

MATT 14:22-36

:22 Gave order, "HIS WILL" ex. didn't say, think about it, you feel like it, form a committee. (Obeyed, did not ask why, did not give their opinion) **:23** If going to minister to people and the impossible must get along with GOD!

:24 **Midst** = middle of performing God's will. Tragedy strikes, storm, tempestuous adversity. **Tossed** = Agitate, tortured, vexed. **Contrary** = against, opposite, opposed, hostile. (wind & storm symbolic of Satan and circumstances) * Try to stop you from doing God's will. *Diametrically opposed to God! Black-white, cold-hot, north-south, day-night, fire-water (Didn't quit, throw in towel, turn around, but pushed on) **PHIL 3:14** I press **:25** 3 o'clock, God's supernatural presence and power came on the scene

:26 Religious, ignorant, superstitious people miss God's blessings. Of the devil -- say. (They have put God in a box) **Fear** = terror, scared, panicked. **:27** Cheer = boldness, courage, merry, "joy of the Lord in strength" **I AM -- the word spoke, killed fear -- :28** Master (of all) must recognize before you'll respond. **:29** Come, it's up to us now! Get out, went against natural upbringing. *Entered supernatural (in Spirit all things possible) Got out and walked, not until Jesus spoke to him. Go beyond self -- "Total dependence on God" -- not self, skill, talent ability, not by power or might, but by spirit and remember the name of the Lord.

:30 Saw wind -- felt regard, take heed to, circumstances, looked at problem.

*Abraham. **ROM 4:9 & 18.** Caused Fear -- Look at Word, cause Faith
Sink. Drown, swallowed up, overwhelm, devourer **I PET 5:8**

:31 Little Faith - Falter, waver, spasmodic, on and off No good reason why to be double minded. **JAMES 1:6** **:33** Did not pat Peter on back, God sustains me just believe. **JOHN 6:21**. Immediately at shore.

MY GRACE IS SUFFICIENT

2 COR 12: 1-10

MAIN ISSUE: Knowledge of God! (Paul) Ever developing knowledge of God. All ways: learning! **:4** Lawful (possible) **:5** I will not glory...! Infirmities: weakness.
:7 Messenger "Angels" 188 times. Angel 181 times. Messengers: 7 times
Buffet: rap with a fist blow after blow. **2 COR 11:23-28**. Blows of Satan
Exalted: God's desire to...

I PET 5:6-7 (MATT 23:12, LUKE 14:11, 18:14) Resist the devil! God only promotes people He can trust. **:8,9** Grace: unmerited favor and ability.
Sufficient: Arkao = content and enough. [1] Raise a barrier [2] Independent [3] Self-sufficient
In weakness: realizes inability so leans on the Lord! Rest: Abide with, take up residence!

HEB 13:5&6 I will not, I will not cease to sustain and uphold you, I will not, I will not, I will not let you down! Count every trial as opportunity to prove God's Word!

GIVE I THEE!

WHERE THE SPIRIT OF THE LORD IS THERE IS LIBERTY "JESUS IS HERE"

ACTS 3:1-8. Man crying out for help "so many" "My life" Hopeless ****If God ever did it once, He will do it again.**

:5 Expecting to receive (most shopping and praying) Supposed to be a believer. **:6** Such as I have -- "Peter had something to give" wasn't pity or sorrow, sympathy or tears, silver or gold, pleasures or riches (something man did not have anything to do with) Before give realize what you have! Many do not know a lot have just enough religion to make miserable. Satan wants to keep blind. Rule where ignorance and unbelief lives!

VISION Did not know who I was (God created-indwelt-empowered-Led) (touch you there touching God) Limitless power in us. Ex: Little old Lady -- 440 Pedal to the metal! "Freedom comes from knowing the truth" *I am and I have.

MATT 10:7&8 Receive power by faith. Jesus came to destroy works of devil.

ACTS 3:6 Name of Jesus (Not by power nor by might) **MARK 16** See yourself as God sees you.

ANOINTING IMPARTED

MR 16:9 Resurrection. Meaning. **ROM 8:11**. But if the Spirit of him that raised up Jesus **MATT 28:18.** All power is **:19** Go ye **LU 10:19** ***Behold, I give unto...*** *Impartation of new life, authority and the anointing. **:10-:11** Believed not ***2 TIM 2:13*** ***If we believe not, yet he abideth faithful: he cannot deny himself***... **:14** Unbelief, hardness, *Ties the hands of God! **:15,:16** Believeth = Saved **(whole)** Not = damned. **:17** Believe, opens up realm of supernatural **:18** Lay hands **(impartation of healing)** **LU 4:40** ***Now when the sun was setting, all they that had any sick with divers diseases brought them unto him; and he laid his hands on everyone of them and healed them.*** *Must come into contact with the resurrected Christ, before we can impart his life. **MR 5:30.** Virtue went out of him.

ACTS 4:31-33

II **ACTS 4:31-33** Great power, witness to resurrection. **5:12** By hands: signs and wonders. Recipients of the light, glory, and power of God. *Silver and gold have I not. ***2 COR 4:7 But we have this treasure in earthen vessels, that the excellency of the power may be of God, and not of us.***

ACTS 19:6

III **ACTS 19:6**. Laid his hands **8:18** Laying on of the apostles hands Holy Ghost was given. **:11-12**. Extraordinary, powers, wonders. **DUET 34:9** Joshua the son of Nun was full of the Spirit of Wisdom for Moses had laid his hands upon him (from Paul's body, virtue, power, tangible. ***I TIM 4:14. Neglect not the gift that is in thee, which was given 2 TIM 1:6 Wherefore, I put thee to remembrance etc.***

FIFTEEN REASONS FOR MIRACLES

I **MATT 4:23-25** Healing all sickness, disease, palsy, possessed etc.

1 Demonstrate God's will. **JHN 6:38** ***For I came down from heaven, not to do mine own will, but the will of Him that sent me... HEB 10:7 Then said, I, lo, I come to do thy will, O God.*** 2 Demonstrates God's power over Satan: ***ACTS 10:38 You know of Jesus of Nazareth who went about ....*** 3 Destroyed Satan's works. ***1 JHN 3:8 For this purpose was the Son of God ...*** 4 Prove God was with Him and us (**ACTS 10:38**) 5 Prove kingdom of God present.

II **MATT 12:28**. **I COR 4:20**. ***For the kingdom of God is not in word, but in power.***

MATT 8:16,17

III **MATT 8:16,17** 6 Demonstrates full salvation for body, soul, and spirit. Salvation is not only for the Spirit of man. 7 Give abundant life **JHN 10:10** 8 **(:17)** Fulfill prophecy 9 Confirms God's sonship, Messianic claim. **JHN 20:30,31** ..... ***But these are written that ye might believe that ye might believe that Jesus is the Christ, the Son of God: and that believing ye might have life through His name.***

10 Glorify's God. **JHN 2:11** ***This beginning of miracles did Jesus in Cana of***

Galilee and manifested forth His glory and did his disciples believed on Him. Makes believers. ***JHN 4:48 Except ye see signs and wonders, ye will not believe.***

MRK 16:15-20

[IV] **MRK 16:15-20** [12]These signs reveal faith [13] **:20** Confirms God's word and love
[14] Sets an example for all Gospel ministers. [15] Reveals the anointing and baptism of Holy Ghost.

ACTS 1:4-8 [1] God's will [2] Power over Satan [3] Destroys Satan [4] God with us. [5] Kingdom present [6] Full salvation [7] Abundant Life [8] Fulfills prophecy [9] Son ship and ambassadors [10] Glorifies God [12] Makes believers [13] Apostles

NO FLESH SHOULD GLORY

(I COR 1:26-31, I COR 2:1-5)

JHN 15:16. Chosen and ordained us! **2:5** "Not to stand in human wisdom or philosophy" We are demonstration -- (Power and glory in the substance and life of a born again believer.) I am a miracle. You are a miracle.

1:27 All are called, but few answer the call! 3 times chosen -- selected Foolish -- dull, stupid, heedless, absurd, silly. I tried to change! "God is in business of making dead men live."**1:29** No flesh, world exalts self, we exalt God. Should glorify God everything we do. **2:2** Jesus Christ, Him Crucified "Supreme Love" Highest mountain, lowest valley, never loose its power. Demonstration of power

1:30 A) Wisdom -- If you have an ounce of brains, you will live for God.
B) Righteousness -- ours as filthy rags rubbish *cleansed by blood "decrees in self like-esteem, confidence. **C)** Sanctification -- set apart, body in line! Walk with God will be different. **D)** Redemption -- Total freedom through cross. Possessed with God! *God needs your permission.

ORDINARY TURNED INTO EXTRAORDINARY

I COR 1:26 - **2:5** **HEB 11:6** **1:26** Few wise, mighty, noble embrace the doctrine of the cross. ***MATT 20:16 The last shall be first, and the first last: For many be called but few chosen***. *A chosen generation. ***JHN 15:16 Ye have not chosen me, but I have chosen and ordained you.*** Qualifications of being used by

God is not determined by the letters -- behind or before your name" On you age, color, or nationality, education! We are living miracles, rainbows, God's neon sign to world.

1:27 Chosen -- selected, picked his choice, option, decided, elected us. (Outcasts, rejects) Foolish, not philosophers, craters, statesmen, nor men of wealth, power or influence. Foolish -- stupid absurd, silly, simpleton's in world's eyes. I was an idiot. The great heart of God pulsates with infinite love for the unlovable. Ex: Me.

Abraham -- God must love the common people, He made so many of them. Confound -- bewilder, perplex, puzzle. **ROM 1:22.** Professing themselves to be wise. They became fools.

PS 8:2* *Out of the mouth of babes and sucklings hast thou ordained praise. :28 Held in contempt, not up to snuff, below their standards. You cannot be anything for until you are nothing. ***ROM 4:17* *Things be not as though they are*.** **:29** No Flesh Glory -- World exalts themselves. Believers exalts God. "Give credit where credit is due"

:30 Traditions and teachings of religion have stolen these blessed truths from the believers. We need to see beyond the misery shadows of this world, into the blessed realm of God's all sufficient kingdom.

Four things Jesus is to us in **2 COR 5:17** and in **ACTS 17:28** God has made us partakers of Himself, through Jesus. (Let God make you what he wants you to be) Ordinary to extraordinary. Caterpillar to butterflies. Unlimited, no boundaries.

EPH 6:10 Not by might, nor by power, but by my spirit, **ZEC 4:6** saith the Lord of Host. **HEB 11:6.** My meat is to do the will of Him who sent. God **JHN 6:57** needs your permission. God needs your permission!

A POT OF OIL

2 KINGS 4:12, 2 COR 3:18, 1 SAM 28:10

[1] **2 KINGS 4:1** Creditor is come = thief, **JHN 10:10 Bondman** = slaves **:2 WHAT HAST THOU?** Take inventory of valuable items! Furniture? House? Talents? Education? No! Oil = anointing, new wine, Holy Ghost. Empty-

uninhabited, vacant, ***HEB 12:1 Lay aside the sin.***

EPH 4:22 That ye put off concerning the former .... (Empty of Self) *** And everything that is not of GOD! Deep consciousness of our nothingness, no confidence in self. **:4 Thou shalt** = specific instructions (God's word tells us what to do) Ex: Elijah and Naaman, dunk seven times! Joshua, Gideon, Jehoshaphat etc:

:5 Vessels = brought, SHUT, = Obedience, (Lord what do you want). *** Obedience better then sacrifice. **Vessels** = Empty & very dry nothing. **Door closed** = personal, intimate.

She Poured = ***ISA 44:3 For I will pour water upon him that is thirsty and floods upon the dry ground. I will pour my Spirit upon thy seed, and my blessings upon they offspring. JOEL 2:28,29 I will pour my Spirit upon all flesh and your sons...*** **ACTS 2:17,18** Pour out filled with His love, joy, faith, anointing, power, presence. **:6 Oil Stayed** = Only flows to the depth of our hunger, emptiness. ** Thimbleful = Ex: Sparrow drinking from ocean, thinks he had it all.

2 COR 3:18

II **2 COR 3:18** ***1 SAM 28:10 For precept must be upon precept, precept upon precept, line upon line. MR 4:28 For the earth bringeth forth fruit of herself, first the blade, then the ear, after that full corn in the ear. PRO 4:18 But the path of the just is as the shining light, that shineth more and more unto the perfect day.*** More of His anointing, love, power, Spirit, blessings, hunger, when you come to let your desire to be simply possessed by Him!

Yielded, yielded more and more until God so possesses us, that from -- our bodies flows his virtue, anointing to a sick and dying world. *Filled with God, filled, filled, filled, and empty of self. **PRO13:24, 22:15, 23:13-14**

SPIRIT POURED OUT -- NUMBER 1

I **ACTS 2:14-21** Prophecy = shall become prophets or will speak God's word under the unction of the Holy Ghost -- drenched. **:18** Pour out = prophecy = Speak the mind, the will, the Word of God. {Ooze with Holy Ghost saturated, sapping} **ISA 10:5** And the glory of the Lord shall be revealed and all flesh will see it together. **Spirit gives supernatural enablement! 9 gifts of the Spirit: Signs, wonders, and conviction. **[Holy Ghost JHN 15, 16, 17]** Flesh = Spirit to affect every area. ***MIC 3:8 But truly I am full of power by the Spirit of the Lord.***

JOEL 2:21-28

II **JOEL 2:21-28 (ACTS 2:17-21)** Previous verse **:21** - Be glad, rejoice **:22** Fruit bearing **:23** Glad, rejoice its going to rain **:24** Full of wheat. "Overflow with Wine and Oil = anointing **:25** Restore **:26** Eat plenty **:27** Ye shall know I am in your midst **ISA 32:9-14** Reveals desolation, thorn, briers, tears, pain. **:15** until the Spirit be poured upon us from on high and the wilderness be a fruitful and the fruitful field be counted a forest! ***PRO 1:23 Behold I will pour out my spirit upon you***. **ZECH 12:10, ISA 44:3, PS 45:2, EZE 39:29**. **Question: If God has and is, why not more affected. **ACTS 10**

III **ACTS 10:34** Peter preaching to Cornelius with kinsmen and friends! **:38** How God anointed Jesus with the Holy Ghost and with power... **:44** Yet spake **:45** Poured out the gift of the Holy Ghost. **:46** Tongues and magnify God **Why?** ***ISA 44:3 I will pour water upon him that is thirsty and floods upon the dry ground. I will pour my Spirit upon thy seed and my blessings upon thine offspring.*** " Hunger and thirst will be filled" **More!** ***PSALM 23:5 thou anointest my head with oil: my cup runneth over***. First: What is the cup? Second: What fills the cup? 2nd question first: Spirit, anointing, gifts, fruits, God's presence, love, joy, peace, goodness ... 1st question, is it your spirit? To some extent yes, ***JHN 7:38 out of your belly shall flow....*** = gush, pour, Holy Ghost.

MR 5:25-30

IV **MR 5:25-30** Virtue gone out = anointing, Spirit **:34** Daughter thy faith {sucked, absorbed, assimilates, draws the anointing, Spirit, God's Glory, His presence} *Faith is a lightning rod! *God's eyes are roaming to an fro. Ex: Abraham, Noah, Moses, Joshua, etc. Faith drinks it in.

Faith is the substance that absorbs the Spirit of God, it is the cup our spiritual man holds and we drink from. "You have to have a cup, before you have a drink!" God pours out upon you to the degree of faith your possessed by. More faith bigger cup, more blessing.

EPH 6:16 Shield of Faith (why shield) it repels unbelief, sin, sickness, poverty. Yet draws attracts God's glory. Unbelief -- repels God's blessings, presence, anointing. [Jesus could heal only a few sick folk in his home town.] Unbelief draws, attracts, like a magnet, sin sickness, God's wrath, etc.

ANOINTED TO PREACH

LUKE 4:18 (Everyone) Because - Preach = Proclaim, declare, broadcast. Three Times, 158 in New Testament. **Gospel -- Good News, Glad Tidings**

*Jesus ministry = preach! Preach -- deliverance (Only method) "Not medicine and doctors, not by works, not with guns, no" Preaching, teaching, and then healing

Why? **ROM 10:17** Faith comes by hearing. "Sent Word and healed." Why most are not healed, won't come to hear!

LUKE 9:1. **LUKE 2&6**. Power and authority through preaching! **1 COR 1:10** "You'll show by your actions what you believe" *Perish -- I know for Lost -- But I'll include unbelieving believers. **Power of God** -- Preaching of cross. (Jesus accomplished.)

TITUS 1:3 Manifested His Word = **(1 PET 2:24, PHIL 4:19)** Through preaching. I preach to myself. Then, faith comes -- It manifests! "Preaching Opens Door for Healing" (More people get healed when hear)

HEB 4:2. Mix Word with Faith You get air by breathing, "Not enough just to believe" You get blessings by believing and acting the Gospel.

IN HIS PRESENCE

I **GEN 3:7&8**. Sinned, heard and hid from the presence of the Lord--God. {Got so caught up in their five physical senses forgot He was there all the time} **Would not sin if aware of His presence! "Acted like was not there" ***1 JHN 3:6 Whosoever abideth in Him sinneth not:*** Practice the presence of God. ***JER 5:22 Fear ye not me? Saith the Lord: Will ye not tremble at my presence, which have placed the sand for the bound of the sea by a perpetual decree, that it cannot pass it and though the waves thereof toss themselves, yet can they not prevail; though they roar, yet can they not pass over it?*** (When the cat is away, the mice will play)

II **GEN 4:16** Cain went out of the presence of the Lord. How? Went the way of the flesh, purposely out of God's will. **JONAH 1:3** Jonah fled from the presence of the Lord! **:10** Storm. It is a dangerous thing to walk out from under God's presence.

ISA 29:15

III **GEN 5:22** Enoch **6:9** Noah **17:1** Abram-walk before me. (Keep yourself before my eyes.) **24:40** Sent servant for wife for Isaac! ***EX 33:14* He said, my presence shall go with thee, I will give thee rest. PS 16:11 In thy presence is fullness of Joy**.

IV **PS 95:1&2**. Thanksgiving will make us aware of His presence **PS 100:1-5**. ***JAMES 4:8* Draw nigh to God and He will draw nigh to you. *JHN 15:4-7* Abide in Him *MATT 28:20* Teaching them to observe all things whatsoever. I have commanded you: and, lo, I am with you always, even unto the end of the world.**

BORN AGAIN -- NUMBER 1

JHN 3:1-8

:3 Except **EPH 2:8** Many people deceived, thinking saved. Born again -- from above, new birth, regenerated, convicted, changed, and transformed. Most Christians do not have the foggiest idea what actually took place. Satan wants to keep up spiritually ignorant, illiterate and blind. Because etc. (Born again million times more then hope -- think or imagine) **EPH 3:20** A necessity -- see, understand, partake, experience. See who you are, "see yourself as God see you -- **:5** Water and Spirit.

EPH 5:26 Washes away sin, sickness, fear, disease. **PS 107:20** Being born again not of corruptible seed, but... **I PET 1:23 JHN 1:12-13** To as many as received him, to them gave He the power.

:6 Two realms (**GEN 1:26 & 2:7**) or dimensions 1) Physical is dominated by physical *Natural man. 2) Spirit is to be dominated by Spirit & Word. *Believer **HEB 10:38** Now **ROM 1:17 GAL 3:11** *Stop trying to act like the world, when you are not of the world.

I COR 1:28 The things which are not bring to nought things that are. You, my friend, through Jesus can subdue and have dominion over your body, mind, emotions, circumstances and situations of life through the name of Jesus.

RIVERS OF LIFE

We are in the midst of a visitation of God and the Holy Ghost.

REV 21. Revelation is a Book of Now for the Body of Christ . It is our wedding march. We are the bride. God is the author of life. Earth is a proto type of heaven.
Earth is clay model of heaven.

THE RIVER OF EDEN

I **JHN 7:37**, Any man thirst, **Drink!** Partake, absorb.

:38 Believe = according to our faith. Flow = flood, abound, to move or express freely, a current. Ex: Cannot see, but under surface. Rivers = a continuous flow, abundance, **Float, flow, move with, do not resist! E: standing in a stream, or on shore of ocean, tide, or waves hitting you. Will take you out into the deep! ***PS 147:18 He sendeth out his word and melteth them: He causeth His wind to blow and the waters to flow.***

II **GEN 2:8,-:10** A river. **1)** Pison = to bring increase, grow up, quicken, {cause word to become alive} **:13 2)** Gihon = Bursting forth or anointing. Ex: Spring near Jerusalem = Soloman anointed and proclaimed king!

:14 3) Hiddekel = Rapid, aggressive, radical, bold, *Kingdon suffereth violence ....
4) Euphrates = fruitfulness, ***JHN 15:8 Here in is my Father gloried, that you bear much fruit***. **EX 2:3**

III **EX 2:3 HEB 11:23** by faith hid, placed into the nile! **:5-6, 10**. Moses -- came from the river! Jesus, led of Holy Ghost, out of the river. **EX 7:20**

IV **EX 7:20** Waters turned blood. ***PS 46:4 There is a river, the streams of which shall make glad the city of God, the Holy place of the tabernacle of the Most High. PS 65:9 The visitest the earth and waterest it. Thou greatly enrichest it with the river of God, which is full of water.***

BLOOD, FIRE, VAPOR OF SMOKE

Manna = What is it? (Bread of heaven) Beyond Concept, how, could, would. *To humble, proud, do good. **JOB 38-41**. God revealed. **:42** Thought he knew God! Admits did not. *Heard before, but now seen! **:6** Wherefore I abhor (despise) myself and repent in dust and ashes. (Cannot know God by mind, emotions, flesh) will have an impact. *Who am I? **MATT 16:16** Art Christ. **:17** Blessed art thou "only by the Spirit" **2 TIM 3:1** Perilous **:5** Form (similitude) of Godliness... *Heard not seen.

I **ACTS 2:1-4**. One of most awesome events in creation! **:16** That **:17** I will, upon all flesh (righteous and unrighteous) rains upon just and unjust. **:18** My Spirit (notice emphasis) Flesh profited. **:21** Whosoever calleth: **(Amp)** invokes, adores, worships. Saved: delivered, made whole, set free. **ACTS 4:12**. There is no other **:19** Blood, fire, vapor: Thick, whirling cloud. God has purpose, reason, plan. *Reality wrapped up in nature, types, shadows. *This is true Christianity! God's plan for man. Way beyond! Ex: Tabernacle in wilderness. *Blood flowed in tabernacle. *Consuming fire above and in (roared, glowed, heat) Tornado of cloud, (covering in and above: Shekinah) (strange, awesome place) What like without blood, fire, vapor of smoke? (Dead formalism) = Modern Christianity. *Not talking manifestations. "Talking reality of Blood, Fire, Vapor of Smoke"

JOEL 2:16

II **JOEL 2:16**. **:23-30** Blood, fire, pillars of smoke. What would a bloodless Christianity be? Lost and undone. ***HEB 9:22 ..... without shedding of blood..... I JHN 1:7 ..... the blood of Jesus Christ hath cleansed.....*** **REV 7:14** Garments made white. ***EPH 2:13 But now in Christ Jesus.... COL 1:20 And having made peace..... ROM 5:9 Much more than, being now justified by his ....*** **ACTS 20:28** Purchased us with **LU 22:20** New testament in my **REV 12:11**. Overcame who's blood? Jesus: Lamb **JHN 10:10** Life. Need blood = need **THE FIRE**

LU 12:49. I am come to send fire on... **EX 3:2** Fire in bush. **EX 19:18**. Lord descended on Sinai in Fire.

PS 97:1-6

III **PS 97:1-6**. **MATT 3:11** Baptize us with Holy Ghost and Fire **HEB 12:29**. Our God is a consuming fire. **ACTS 2:3** Cloven tongues **HEB 1:7** Ministries **PS 39:3**. While I was musing the fire burned. ***JER 20:9 His Word was in my heart as a burning fire.*** If need blood, fire, then vapor of smoke. **:2** Clouds (Shekinah) Told Moses **EX 19:9**. I come unto thee in a thick cloud. **JOB 37:11** Till he weareth the thick cloud. **ISA 19:1**. Rideth upon a swift cloud. **PS 104:3**

Clouds are his chariots. ***MATT 17:5* A bright cloud over shadowed them** (transfigure) **I COR 10:2** All were baptized unto Moses in the cloud and in the sea! *Someone says do not need blood. We say no way! How about fire and vapor of smoke. *God's nature, essence, character. In the tabernacle. In us! Takes faith to apply! All three.

SPIRIT OF PREACH

LUKE 4:18-19

LUKE 4:16-17 (Holy Spirit) To preach (More in three years than anything else.) **Preaching, teaching, and then miracles and healings? Miracles happen when the Word is preached.

LUKE 1:17 Spirit of Elisha (to preach repentance) *More important then sign. Noah -- preacher of righteousness. Most old testament saints were!

JHN 15:26 **JHN 16:13** Give witness to Jesus. (Same job when in us) **JHN 3:34** Without measure, to preach! "**US TO**" (Holy Ghost) Stay under the fountain of Life. Ex: Old Faithful (Geyser)

ACTS 1:8 Some Spirit !!! **ACTS 2:17-18.** Prophesy (Speak form by divine inspiration) "Power of God is released through the Gospel" **1 COR 1:18-21** Word is lifeless until faith is breathed into it on your lips!

SPIRIT OF THE LORD IS UPON US TO PREACH!

THE WHY OF TONGUES

I COR 12:4-7 Three dimensions of Body

TONGUES Supernatural utterance inspired by God in an unknown tongue. It is a New Testament experience that is distinctive to this generation; and yet it has become one of the most controversial and misunderstood subjects of the Bible. (There are those who say it's done away with. **I COR 13:8-10** Ridicules. As long as on this side of heaven, it will not cease. (Those who say insignificant) **I**

COR 14:18 Did more than all, **14:5** wished that. Devil hates because of potentiality and power that is released through this Gift! **I COR 14** - Paul was not disclaiming but instructing.

10 MAJOR REASONS

1) MR 16:17 These signs, evidence of the presence and power of Holy Ghost (authenticates, substantiates, verifies God's presence.) **I COR 14:22** - Fire by night, cloud by day. **ACTS 2:3 & 4** -- Replaced with tongues. Proof to the World.

2) A supernatural means of communicating directly to God. An umbilical cord of divine fellowships **I COR 14:2 & 27,28** * Also, the devil does not understand, therefore cannot interfere (but in) hinder or obstruct your prayers like he did to Daniel.

3) Can pray the perfect mind and will of God **ROM 8:26 & 27.** (He who knows all things, can pray through us about things which our natural mind knows nothing about.) *Eliminated the possibility of selfishness entering into our prayers, or wrong praying which is out of line with the Word and the will of God!

4) Provides a way of praise and thanksgiving to God. **I COR 14:15 & 17**

5) Helps us to become God inside conscious, which is bound to effect the way I live. "We have a tendency of forgetting the Greater One in us."

6) Spiritual edifies us, not physical or mental. **I COR 14:4** (Enriches, cultivates, develops, improves us spiritually) *Out of your belly - a flowing stream that should never dry up.

7) **ISA 28:11,12** -- rest, refreshment, from turmil, perplexity, insecurity, (tranquility, relaxation, vacation, restores, revives, renews) -- A tremendous pick-me-up

8) **JUDE 20** - Charges, fortifies your faith. Stimulates, invigorates. *One of the greatest spirtiual exercies there is. Takes faith to pray in, believe it is accomplishing, etc. Prepares us for whatever the future holds in store for us. Gets us ready.

9) Keeps our bodies under the control of the Holy Spirt.

JAMES 3:2-4 Tongue is rudder and bridle of.

10) Teaches you how to yield yourself to God, thereby opening the door for the other gifts to flow.

"KEY TO MANIFESTATION OF GIFTS"

TRANSFERRING THE ANOINTING

ACTS 19:11-12, 2 KINGS 13:20,21, MATT 9:20 -- 2 KINGS 2:8, 13 & 14

Special miracles (extraordinary wonders) healed, devils driven out, made to go. *From His Body! (anointing imparted into cloth) conveyed, transmitted, tangible, material, real, perceptible. *Many kinds of power or energy. **2 KINGS 13:20,21** The virtue, power of God was still in Elisha's bones. Anointing = Capacitor - ability to absorb and contain. It communicated life to a dead body *More we die to ourselves more. **MATT 9:20-22** (**MR 6:53:56** Border) How did she know? **NUM 15:38-41** -ribbon of blue **(MATT 14:34-36)** perceived, tangible

DEUT 22:12 Fringes on the four quarters (wings) of they restore. **MAL 4:2** But unto you that fear my name shall the Son of righteousness arise with healing in His wings: **EX 25:20** Wings are a representative of God's presence, mercy, power

2 KINGS 2:8 13 & 14 Anointing of Elijah transmitted to Elisha (Lay hands on no man suddenly) *Mantle **ACTS 5:15** Shadow of Peter healed the sick ***3:1-8** As I have (not natural, emotional, financial) **Anointing** = transferable, transmit, convey, impart. *Believe you have and can **I JHN 2:27** **ACTS 10:38** **GAL 3:5**

The same miracle working power that was in Jesus, is now in us! ***HAVE TO RELEASE THE ANOINTING IN YOU!***

VISITATIONS OF GOD -- NUMBER 1

I JHN 5: Some said not happen, not of God, natural cure. (Bible is Bible) **:1**

Passover feast, Jesus, in Jerusalem. **:2** Sheep Gate, Bethesda = Mercy {A place of mercy} Great multitude -- afflicted, sick, hurting, diseased, (today's generation) *Do not know their sick! Waiting = hoping, begging, wishing something would happen, help, moving stirring, agitation, quickening) **Supernatural, miracles, divine happening. Not devil, demons, satanic, new age, or natural -- was a visitation from heaven. **:4** Angel -- angelic visitation, divine house call, sovereign move, God showing up.

Not at 1st **GEN 3:8** and they heard the voice of the Lord walking in the garden, in the...why? Walk, visit, fellowship. Ex: Enoch, Noah, Abraham, Jacob, Joseph, Moses etc. **PS 8:4** What is man, that thou art mindful of him? and the Son of man, that thou visitest him? Season-now and then-unpredictable [cannot tell when God is going to move] Troubled stirred {God must first stir the hearts of men} **Impregnated the water with healing, virtue, tangible anointing. First step: into the move, visitation. **Angel stir, but they had to respond.

WHATSOEVER brought healing, deliverance, wholeness. Major problem: not enough for everyone. **:5** 38 years -hoping, praying **:6** Jesus = who? Immanuel -- God with us, word made flesh. Come to earth. **GAL 4:4** But when the fullness ... *Visitation of the Lord {walked through crowds did not know a visitation of God} **LU 1:78** The Dayspring from high hath visited us. Did not have to be sick any more. WILT thou = looking for those who will receive. **:7** Explains would but cannot! **:8** Rise = **LU 19:10** for the Son of Man is come to seek and to save that which is lost. **:9** Immediately. **JHN 4:14**. Step into the water and drink

LU 5:17

II **LU 5:17** Power = anointing, virtue, presence. To heal them {man with palsy} Divine Sovereign move, visitation. **MR 6:5** And he could there do no mighty work. Save that he laid his hands upon a few sick folk and healed them. [King of Kings, Author of Life, Alpha and Omega -- would not step into the water]

MUST 1) Be desperate, hungry. **2)** At right place, geographically and Spirit. **3)** Right time. **4)** Step in, by actions, confession.

ACTS 5:14

III **ACTS 5:14-16**. Healed everyone -- All four elements involved! Throughout history visitations of God. 1500 Reformation (Martin Luther) 1800 [Wesley Finney, Moody, Tailor] 1904 Welsh, Asuzo Street 1930 [Amy,Wigglesworth, Lake, Dowey]
1950 Healing 1970 Charismatic 1990 **NOW** *The water is stirring. God visiting.

Holy Ghost touching. Jesus is healing. [1] Desperate [2] Right place [3] Right time [4] Step in

WALKING ON THE WATER

MATT 14:22-33

MATT 14:24. Tossed = Torture vex contrary = against, opposite waves is daily circumstances, wind is the devil. **MATT 14:25** Walking = To trample down under foot for Jesus walking above, not below circumstances.

MATT 14:26. A lot of Christians afraid of tongues and gifts. **MATT 14:27** Cheer: Have courage boldness (daring) It is I that is setting the captives free.

Isaiah 41:10 ***Fear thou not; for I am with thee: be not dismayed; for I am thy God: I will strengthen thee; yea, I will help thee; yea, I will uphold thee with the right hand of my righteous.***

MATT 14:28 Bid: Order, command Peter says is Your will then tell me, is it God's will we are healed? etc. **MATT 14:29** Come. Bible tells us so! Once you know God's will. **ACT!**

JAMES 1:22-24 Doer. Keep your eyes on the word of God. Look to Jesus the Author and Finisher of our Faith. Peter trampled under foot: the circumstances!

MATT 14:30. Saw: regard, take heed. Peter saw wind. Took eyes of Jesus and listened to devil. Then fear moves in, and Peter began to sink. When you start walking by Faith, keep your eyes on the Word and not the circumstances. Praise God, just in time Peter cried out and put his eyes back on Jesus or circumstances would have drowned him.

MATT 14:31. Get back on the Word, will receive help immediately. Little: Lacking confidence in Jesus. Wherefore: reached or entered. Peter didn't have to doubt. All you need is Faith the size of mustard seed.

JAMES 1:5 ***If any of you lack wisdom let him ask of God, ...*** ***JAMES 1:6-7.*** ***For he that wavereth is like a wave of the sea driven with the wind and tossed. For let not that man think that he shall receive any thing of the Lord.***

MATT 14:32. Wind ceased. Slowly diminished. Resist the devil and he shall flee. Always going to be trials because we are in the world. **MATT 14:33**

Overcome and it will glorify God.

ANOINTING WITHIN

[I] **JHN 3:7&8 Purpose** = reason, cause, end. **Manifested** = **<u>I TIM 3:16</u>** with **Destroy** = obliterate, put an end, undo. (What works?_ **<u>JHN 10:10</u>**) **<u>EPH 6:12</u>** *Did succeed? **COL 2:15** Overcame_ **<u>MATT 28:18</u>** All power How?_ ***<u>2 COR 10:4</u> Weapons of our warfare.....*** ***ANOINTING** = ***<u>ISA 10:27</u> Yoke is destroyed because .... <u>ACTS 10:38</u> How God anointed .....*** *The works that I do, how? Anointing.

I JHN 2:20

[II] **I JHN 2:20 UNCTION** = an anointing *If the same...that raised... ****<u>LU 4:18</u> The spirit of the Lord*** = anointing = source, origin, essence of our success. ***<u>I PET 4:11</u> If any man minister let him do it as....*** [God has provided]

I JHN 2:27

[III] **I JHN 2:27** In you (after baptized in Holy Ghost) ***<u>ACTS 1:8</u> Receive power, after Holy Ghost***. Ex: Seed, **child** = awesome potential. {Man not teacher -- Holy Ghost by *anointing = five fold} Taught to abide! Intimate fellowship. *Anointings can only teach and flow to the extent you believe, obey, allow God and his word to control life.

LU 6:17-19

[IV] **LU 6:17-19** Sought = struggled. **VIRTUE** = Power, anointing, life of God -- creative ability. Ex: Lightning rod *vessel, container, capacitor [recipients of the light, glory, anointing, power of God] (16 buckets water, 1 mud) *Carry around a certain spirit! Presence Ex: James, John. Know not what spirit of Son of God came not condemn, but might have life. Ex: cup-dip in = ful of

LU 8:43-46

[V] **LU 8:43-46** Virtue flowed = power, anointing, life, light, glory *She dipped her cup into his well\out of you belly - whatever it is full of. *Anointing is received and released by what you
[I] Hear, [II] See [III] Believe [IV] Act

Some of the Books Written by Doc Yeager:

"Living in the Realm of the Miraculous #1"

"I need God Cause I'm Stupid"

"The Miracles of Smith Wigglesworth"

"How Faith Comes 28 WAYS"

"Horrors of Hell, Splendors of Heaven"

"The Coming Great Awakening"

"Sinners In The Hands of an Angry GOD", "(modernized)"

"Brain Parasite Epidemic"

"My JOURNEY To HELL" - illustrated for teenagers

"Divine Revelation Of Jesus Christ"

"My Daily Meditations"

"Holy Bible of JESUS CHRIST"

"War In The Heavenlies - (Chronicles of Micah)"

"Living in the Realm of the Miraculous #2"

"My Legal Rights To Witness"

"Why We (MUST) Gather!- 30 Biblical Reasons"

"My Incredible, Supernatural, Divine Experiences"

"Living in the Realm of the Miraculous #3"

"How GOD Leads & Guides! - 20 Ways"

ABOUT THE AUTHOR

Dr. Michael and Kathleen Yeager have served as pastors/apostles, missionaries, evangelists, broadcasters and authors for over four decades. They flow in the gifts of the Holy Spirit, teaching the Word of God with wonderful signs and miracles following in confirmation of God's Word. In 1983, they began Jesus is Lord Ministries International, Biglerville, PA 17307.

Websites Connected to Doc Yeager

www.docyeager.com

www.jilmi.org

www.wbntv.org

Printed in Great Britain
by Amazon

12916479R00113